The Leading Lawyer

A Guide to Practicing Law and Leadership

ROBERT W. CULLEN

THOMSON
＊ ™
WEST

This publication was created to provide you with accurate and author-itative information concerning the subject matter covered; however, this publication was not necessarily prepared by persons licensed to practice law in a particular jurisdiction. The publisher is not engaged in rendering legal or other professional advice and this publication is not a substitute for the advice of an attorney. If you require legal or other expert advice, you should seek the services of a competent attor-ney or other professional.

ISBN 978-0-314-99614-5

ACKNOWLEDGEMENTS

For those who were involved and helped shape the events and opportunities leading up to, and during, the writing of this book, I am sincerely thankful.

First, and foremost, I am indebted to the Leading Lawyers, who allowed me to interview them, for their graciousness, wisdom and inspiration. They gave up valuable time, told indispensable stories, and provided sage insights that make it clear that leadership is essential to success in the legal profession and to the improvement of the communities in which we work and live.

With respect to my own pathway of practicing law, mediation, teaching, and now writing, I thank my old firm, Hoge, Fenton, Jones, and Appel, Inc. I am proud to say that the idea of community service and dedication to our legal community was instilled in me by my partners and peers. I am grateful for the influence of the lawyers and professional staff who were a main part of my experience at Hoge, Fenton. During my 18 years of practicing law with these men and women of character, they taught me the principles of professionalism and integrity; principles that I try to pass on to my students and continue to personally strive to embody today.

I am also thankful for the support of Donald Polden, Dean at Santa Clara University School of Law and Cynthia Mertens, Associate Dean of Academics. They have been instrumental in focusing on leadership at the law school and have been very supportive of my work. I further appreciate the assistance of Barry Posner, Dean of the Business School at Santa Clara University and leadership expert extraordinaire, whose model of academic excellence I have attempted to emulate. I was, and am continually, inspired by the host of other great people at Santa Clara that are dedicated to it's mission of "competence, conscience and compassion."

I am especially thankful to all my students that contributed to the book. Their research and hard work helped my efforts tremendously. I am most appreciative of my law clerk Erin John; she gave me incredible assistance and overall energy during the summer of 2008, which helped me drive the book to conclusion.

I also owe a great debt of gratitude to Susan Vogel and Richard Hardack who provided much needed guidance and wisdom along the way. Also, Sarah Carter and Jennifer Hummel have been invaluable in helping with many details and have provided great support.

Furthermore, one cannot go through any important experience without remembering those who helped pave the way. A sincere and special thanks for so many things to my parents, Frances and my late father, Rob, for their unconditional love and support through all my years; my sisters, Carol and Jean and their families. I am also very lucky to have great in-laws; thank you to my mother-in-law Fay Lim whose kindness is unmatched and my two brothers-in-law, Bob and Ben, who I greatly appreciate.

Lastly, I am most thankful for my wife and partner, June, with whom my life has been lovingly shared for the last 20 plus years. Her support has been unending and without her my life would not be the same. She and our two wonderful children, Cari and Christie, are my sources of love, happiness and affection. They are simply what keep me going.

Thanks everyone,

Bob Cullen

PREFACE

This book came about as a result of my desire to show my law students what skills and attributes make a lawyer successful. I have been teaching at the Law School at Santa Clara University for 10 years and my students careers were always a priority for me. So, when I initially set out to learn more about the skill sets, characteristics and traits common among the most successful lawyers, I had no intention of using the information in a book. I began my inquiries out of simple curiosity and a desire to teach my students something about the legal profession that they wouldn't get by reading and analyzing appellate cases.

In my 25 years as a lawyer, manger of a law firm and a mediator, along with my research into leadership, I began to determine that leadership, in any profession or sector, is the common denominator for an exceptional career. But I asked myself: What can I teach my students about leadership that they can use in their careers as lawyers? I began to perform more in-depth academic research and also started talking to lawyers who are successful, not only in their firms and organizations, but are leaders in their fields, the profession, their communities and are also facilitators of positive change. After speaking with many influential and successful lawyers, I began to realize that their stories shared common themes, and beyond that, they were all satisfied and fulfilled by their work and grateful for the career opportunities that they felt were available to them because they were lawyers. I started to see that the stories, insights, and advice that these leaders provided should be offered to my students as more than a footnote to some of the classes I was teaching but should be a course unto its own. Now my class Leadership for Lawyers is being offered in its fourth year at Santa Clara with great support from the Law School and the Dean, Donald Polden.

When I decided to turn my research and findings into a book, I created a list of people that I wanted to interview. The list changed slightly over time because of schedules and accessibility but I wanted to obtain interviews with lawyers from a wide variety of industries: non-profit and for-profit corporations, a government and non-governmental agency, litigators, politicians, business lawyers and the judiciary. I relied upon suggestions from other lawyers and my own research. While I am very pleased with my list of Leading Lawyers and am deeply grateful for their time, wisdom and invaluable insights, I am aware that one can just as easily come up with ten different Leading Lawyers from an even more diverse cross-section of industries. However, if you were to interview ten *different* Leading Lawyers, then I believe you will get ten *similar* opinions regarding integrity, credibility, drive, and the additional skill sets necessary to become a Leading Lawyer. I was not only moved by many of their stories, but I was also struck by the way each of them spoke of integrity with such passion as well their high level of commitment to the legal profession.

After this project, I am far more optimistic about the direction of the legal profession and even more proud to be a part of it.

Robert W. Cullen

BIOGRAPHIES

ELIZABETH J. CABRASER, is a founding partner of Lieff, Cabraser, Heimann & Bernstein, LLP. She is an attorney with 30 years experience representing plaintiffs in securities and investment fraud, consumer fraud, product liability, toxic contamination, employment discrimination, and civil rights litigation, in federal and state courts across the country.

Her litigation, trial and settlement experience includes work for plaintiffs in breast implant cases, diet drug cases, Holocaust litigation as well as tobacco litigation. She has served as court-appointed lead or co-lead counsel in over 80 federal multidistrict and state coordinated proceedings, including lead or co-lead counsel roles in eight major multidistrict securities litigations. Ms. Cabraser has also participated in the design, structure and conduct of eight nationwide class action trials in securities fraud, product liability, mass accident and consumer cases in state and federal courts.

Ms. Cabraser received her A.B. in 1975 and her J.D. in 1978, both from the University of California at Berkeley. She has written scholarly and practical articles and lectured extensively. Ms. Cabraser has served as Visiting Professor of Law at Columbia University and Adjunct Professor of Law at the University of California, Berkeley (Boalt Hall). She currently teaches an advanced class actions seminar at Boalt Hall. She has also lectured for the Federal Judicial Center, ALI-ABA, the National Center for State Courts, Vanderbilt University Law School, and the Practicing Law Institute. Her recent legal publications are extensive and include the treatise *California Class Action Practice and Procedure*; and the articles "The Manageable Nationwide Class: A Choice-of-Law Legacy of *Phillips Petroleum Co. v. Shutts*," "The Class Action Counterreformation," "Human Rights Violations As Mass Torts: Compensation As A Proxy For Justice In The United States Civil Litigation System," and many more.

Ms. Cabraser was appointed in 1994 to serve on the California Constitution Revision Commission, and, in 1996, on the California Senate Special Task Force on Shareholder Litigation. She also serves on the American Law Institute (ALI) Council.

She is the recipient of the Consumer Attorneys of California's 1998 Presidential Award of Merit for her commitment to consumer protection and the Anti-Defamation League's Distinguished Jurisprudence Award for her work in the federal Holocaust Litigation in 2002. She also received the 2006 Distinguished Leadership Award from the Legal Community Against Violence, and the University of San Francisco School of Law's 2007 Award for Public Interest Excellence. She has been named repeatedly as one of *The National Law Journal's* 100 Most Influential Lawyers in America, and one of the journal's 50 Most Influential Women Lawyers and Top Ten Women Litigators.

DEBORAH A. GARZA is a highly accomplished attorney and a national authority in antitrust law. She currently serves as the Deputy Assistant Attorney General for Regulatory Matters in the Antitrust Division of the Department of Justice. Her duties vest authority to oversee regulatory matters in the Transportation, Energy and Agriculture, and Telecommunications and Media Sections, as well as other regulatory matters for the Division. In 2004, Ms. Garza was appointed by President Bush to chair the Antitrust Modernization Commission (AMC), a bipartisan panel created by Congress to evaluate and make recommendations on United States antitrust laws and policy. The AMC issued its highly praised report to the President and Congress in 2007.

Ms. Garza held two positions with the Department of Justice prior to her current position. From 1988 to 1989 she served as chief of staff in the Antitrust Division and from 1984 to 1985 she served as a special assistant to the Assistant Attorney General.

Prior to rejoining the Department of Justice, Ms. Garza was a partner in two different firms practicing antitrust law. In 2001, she joined the antitrust law practice of Fried, Frank, Harris, Shriver & Jacobson, LLP in Washington, D.C. and from 1989 to 2001, Ms. Garza was a partner at Convington & Burling. During her private practice, Ms. Garza engaged in a wide range of antitrust counseling and litigation matters with a particular focus on mergers and acquisitions, including transactions in the transportation, energy, telecommunications and high-tech industries. Some of the high-profile mergers in which Ms. Garza has provided antitrust counsel include the merger of Exxon and Mobil; ConocoPhillips' acquisition of Burlington Resources, Inc.; MGM Mirage's purchase of the Mandalay Resort Group; and USAirways' merger with America West. Ms. Garza also served on the trial team representing the National Football League in its antitrust fight with the United States Football League.

Ms. Garza received her B.S. from Northern Illinois University in 1978 and her J.D. from the University of Chicago Law School in 1981.

ROBERT J. GREY, JR. is a partner in the Richmond, Virginia office of Hunton & Williams where he focuses on administrative matters before state and federal agencies, mediation and dispute resolution, and legislative representation of clients. He was previously a partner at the firm LeClair Ryan and co-founder of the firm Grey & Wesley.

Mr. Grey served as President of the American Bar Association from 2005 to 2006 and devoted his yearlong term to creating better justice through better juries via the American Jury Initiative. The Jury Initiative was composed of the Commission on the American Jury and the American Jury Project. The Commission was dedicated to educating the public on, and reinvigorating the nation's commitment to, jury service. The American Jury Project modernized and consolidated varying sets of juror standards into a single model document that reflects the demands of contemporary trials. Mr. Grey also worked to review, unify and update ABA programs to increase diversity in the legal profession, to advance the ABA's international rule of law efforts, and to safeguard the profession's independence.

Mr. Grey has long been an active member of the ABA. From 2000 to 2002 Mr. Grey chaired the Committee on Research about the Future of the Legal Profession, which analyzed trends affecting the practice of law and identified steps the profession should take to preserve and advance its fundamental values. From 1998 to 2000, he chaired the policy-making House of Delegates. He has also been active in strategic planning and increasing diversity in the legal profession. From 1992 to 1995 he also chaired the Commission on Opportunities for Minorities in the Profession. Previous to that, he chaired the Virginia delegation in the ABA House of Delegates and the Commission in Opportunities for Minorities in the Profession.

Mr. Grey earned his law degree from Washington and Lee University in 1976. He has received several gubernatorial appointments including chair of the Virginia Alcoholic Beverage Control Board, vice chair of the Virginia Public Building Authority, and member of the Virginia Polytechnic Institute and State University Board of Visitors. Mr. Grey was also the recipient of numerous awards, including the Thurgood Marshall College Fund Award of Excellence and the Distinguished Leadership Award from the National Association for Community Leadership, the Alumni Star Award from Virginia Commonwealth University School of Business, and the Gertrude E. Rush and Wiley A. Branton Awards from the National Bar Association.

RUDOLPH W. GIULIANI received his J.D. degree, *cum laude*, from New York University Law School in 1968 and his B.A. from Manhattan College in 1965. Upon graduation, he clerked for District Court Judge Lloyd MacMahon. In 1970, he joined the office of the US Attorney and five years later was recruited to Washington, D.C. as Associate Deputy Attorney General and chief of staff to the Deputy Attorney General. He returned to New York to practice law at Patterson, Belknap, Webb & Tyler from 1977 to 1981. In 1981, Mr. Giuliani was named Associate Attorney General, the third highest position in the Department of Justice. Two years later, he was appointed US Attorney for the Southern District of New York, where he spearheaded the effort to jail drug dealers, fight organized crime, break the web of corruption in government, and prosecute white-collar criminals. Few US Attorneys in history can match his record of 4,152 convictions with only 25 reversals.

After an impressive career as a government prosecutor, Mr. Giuliani was elected as the 107th mayor of New York City in 1993. In 1997, he was re-elected by a wide margin, carrying four out of New York City's five boroughs. Under Mr. Giuliani's leadership, New York City implemented innovative strategies for reducing crime, reforming welfare, encouraging economic growth, and improving overall quality of life. Mr. Giuliani's leadership played an indispensable role following the September 11, 2001 attacks on the World Trade Center in New York City.

After serving as mayor, Mr. Giuliani founded Giuliani Partners, a consulting firm based in New York, in January 2002. He later joined the Bracewell & Giuliani law firm. In 2008, Mr. Giuliani ran for the Republican Party nomination for president. After leading in national polls early in the campaign, he withdrew to endorse Senator John McCain.

Mr. Giuliani is the recipient of several prestigious awards and acknowledgments. In 1998, while mayor, he received The Hundred Year Association of New York's Gold Medal Award in recognition of outstanding contributions to the City. In recognition of his leadership on and after the September 11 attacks, Queen Elizabeth II granted him honorary knighthood and *Time* magazine named Mr. Giuliani Person of the Year for 2001. In 2002, the Episcopal Diocese of New York gave Mr. Giuliani the Fiorello LaGuardia Public Service Award for Valor and Leadership in the Time of Global Crisis. That same year, former First Lady Nancy Reagan awarded him the Ronald Reagan Freedom Award. Mr. Giuliani has received honorary degrees from Loyola College and Middlebury College as well as an honorary Doctorate in Public Administration from The Citadel. He authored the book *Leadership*, published in 2002.

BEN W. HEINEMAN, JR. is currently senior counsel at WilmerHale in Washington, D.C. and Distinguished Senior Fellow at Harvard Law School's Program on the Legal Profession. He is also a senior fellow at the Belfer Center for Science and International Affairs at Harvard's Kennedy School of Government. He serves on the board of the center for Strategic and International Studies, the Memorial Sloan Kettering Cancer Center, Transparency International-USA and The National Constitution Center.

Perhaps Mr. Heineman is best known for his long years of service as General Electric's senior vice president and general counsel from 1987 until 2003. He also served as GE's vice president for law and public affairs from 2004 until his retirement in 2005. While at GE, he was responsible for managing a team of 1,100 in-house attorneys in over 100 countries around the world. During his tenure, GE's legal department gained world recognition for its excellence in legal, business and management service.

Mr. Heineman is a Harvard College and Oxford University graduate as well as a Rhodes Scholar. After receiving his Juris Doctor degree from Yale Law School, where he was editor-in-chief of the *Yale Law Journal*, he served as a law clerk to Supreme Court Justice Potter Stewart from 1971 until 1972.

Mr. Heineman began his legal career as a staff attorney for the Center for Law & Social Policy in Washington, D.C. and then became a litigator at Williams & Connolly. He later served as assistant secretary for policy at the Department of Health, Education, and Welfare from 1977 until 1980 under President Carter. Prior to joining General Electric, Mr. Heineman was also managing partner of the Washington, D.C. office of Sidley & Austin, focusing on Supreme Court and test case litigation.

He researches and writes on a variety of topics, including globalization, anticorruption, corporate citizenship, dispute resolution, and the legal profession. Mr. Heineman is the author of books on British race relations and the American presidency. He is also the author of the recent book, *High Performance with High Integrity* published in the spring of 2008. His list of honors and awards include the 2008 Lifetime Achievement Award from *Corporate Board Member Magazine*, inclusion in *The National Law Journal's* list of "The 100 Most Influential Lawyers in America" in 2006, and the National Legal Aid and Defenders Association Exemplar Award in 2004.

JUSTICE JOYCE L. KENNARD is an Associate Justice on the Supreme Court of California. She was born in a Japanese concentration camp to a Dutch father and Chinese-Indonesian mother during World War II. In 1961, at the age of 20, she immigrated to the United States alone. Continuing her effort to obtain an education, she worked part-time as a secretary in order to support herself through her undergraduate and professional studies. In 1974, she earned her J.D. and M.P.A from the University of Southern California, from where she also obtained her B.A. degree Phi Beta Kappa.

After graduating from law school, Justice Kennard served as Deputy Attorney General in Los Angeles. Following her years in the State's attorney general office, Justice Kennard rose quickly within the California court system. In 1986 she was appointed to the Los Angeles Municipal Court. One year later, she was elevated to the California Superior Court and in 1988 to the California Court of Appeal. Then, in 1989, Governor Deukmejian appointed her to the California Supreme Court, where she was the second woman, and first Asian-American, to serve as a justice on the Court. She is currently the longest serving justice sitting on the Court, having been retained by voters in 1994 and again in 2006.

While on the California Supreme Court, Justice Kennard chaired the California Judicial Council's Appellate Advisory Committee from 1996-2005. She also oversaw a six-year project to simplify the wording and clarify the meaning of the rules of the California Supreme Court and Courts of Appeal. Justice Kennard is well known for her dissents, firmly believing that opposing views within the court should be expressed and heard. She is also known for her thorough questioning during oral argument.

She has been the recipient of many awards, including the Alumni Merit Award from the University of Southern California School of Policy, Planning, and Development and the Emil Gumpert ADR Judicial Services Award from the Dispute Resolution Services, Inc. Justice Kennard was also the recipient of the 2007 Lifetime Achievement Award from the Queen's Bench; the 2006 Lifetime Achievement Award from the Japanese American Bar Association of Greater Los Angeles, the 2001 Bird Memorial Award from the California Women Lawyers; and the 1991 Justice of the Year Award from the California Trial Lawyers Association. Justice Kennard has received honorary doctor of laws degrees from the University of Southern California, San Joaquin College of Law, and Lewis & Clark's Northwestern School of Law, Lincoln Law School, Whittier Law School, Southwestern University School of Law, California Western School of Law and Pepperdine School of Law.

FRED KRUPP has served as president of the Environmental Defense Fund (EFD), a nonprofit environmental advocacy group, since 1984. As the head of EFD, he has been instrumental in developing many innovative market-based solutions to environmental problems. These include the acid rain reduction plan in the 1990 Clean Air Act and the United States proposal to achieve least-cost greenhouse gas reduction in the Kyoto Protocol. Mr. Krupp broke new ground by engaging American companies to lessen their impact on the environment. Strategic partnerships with McDonald's, FedEx, and DuPont, among others, have resulted in the elimination of millions of pounds of waste, the adoption of hybrid delivery vehicles, and an accord to reduce the environmental risks of nanotechnology. He also helped launch a corporate coalition, the U.S. Climate Action Partnership, whose Fortune 500 members—Alcoa, BP, Caterpillar, GE and dozens more—have called for strict limits on global warming pollution.

Prior to his work at EFD, Mr. Krupp was a partner in private practice with Albis & Krupp from 1978 to 1984. During that time he also founded and served as general counsel for the Connecticut Fund for the Environment, a leading state environmental group. In 1984, he was also a partner in Cooper, Whitney, Cochran & Krupp in 1984.

Mr. Krupp currently serves on the board of the H. John Heinz III Center for Science, Economics and the Environment; the John F. Kennedy School of Government Environment Council; and the Leadership Council of the Yale School of Forestry and Environmental Studies. He has also served on the President's Advisory Committee on Trade Policy and Negotiations for Presidents Bill Clinton and George W. Bush.

A New Jersey native, Mr. Krupp earned his undergraduate degree from Yale University and his J.D. from the University of Michigan. He has taught environmental law at both universities and is co-author of the book *Earth: The Sequel*, a *New York Times* Best Seller. In recognition of his environmental work, he was the recipient of the 1999 Keystone Leadership in Environment Award; the 2002 Champion Award from the Women's Council on Energy and the Environment; and in 2007 was among 16 people named America's Best Leaders by *U.S. News and World Report*.

WILLIAM T. LORIS is co-founder of the International Development Law Organization and has served as Director-General of the organization since 2001. Mr. Loris helped found the IDLO in 1983 as a Dutch foundation and in 1988 it was re-founded as an intergovernmental organization by means of multilateral convention. In 2001, the United Nations General Assembly granted the IDLO permanent observer status. The IDLO provides tools and skills to establish and maintain the rule of law and good governance within developing countries, countries in economic transition and countries emerging from armed conflict. It provides training, technical assistance, research and publication to governments, non-governmental organizations, local communities and professional associations.

Mr. Loris has dedicated his entire career to addressing the legal aspects of development. Under his leadership, the IDLO has played a key role in peacebuilding reconstruction in Afghanistan, Timor-Leste, the Democratic Republic of Congo and Kosovo. Mr. Loris has also initiated efforts to assist the governments of Indonesia and Sri Lanka to structure an emergency program of legal assistance for the victims of the 2004 tsunami. Mr. Loris has spearheaded numerous assistances programs for African countries to develop legislation designed to ensure women and children who are spared from the HIV/AIDS pandemic enjoy full inheritance of property rights.

Mr. Loris earned his J.D. from Santa Clara University School of Law and a Masters degree in International and Comparative Law from Vrije Universiteit in Brussels. Prior to the IDLO, he worked for 11 years in Africa and the Middle East with the United States Agency for International Development (USAID), first as Regional Legal Advisor for West and Central Africa based in the Ivory Coast and later as the Legal Advisor for the USAID Mission in Egypt.

LEON E. PANETTA is the co-founder and co-director of the Leon & Sylvia Panetta Institute for Public Policy. The institute was created to provide a variety of study opportunities in government, politics and public policy, and sponsor a range of other activities to benefit its surrounding communities.

Mr. Panetta attended Santa Clara University where he earned his B.A degree in 1960 and J.D. in 1963. Upon graduation, he joined the United States Army as a Second Lieutenant. Mr. Panetta received the Army Commendation Medal and was discharged as a Captain in 1966. After his military service, he served as legislative assistant to Senator Thomas Kuchel of California, the Senate Minority Whip. In 1969 he became assistant to Robert H. Finch, the Secretary of Health, Education and Welfare. Soon after, he was appointed Director of the Office for Civil Rights where he chose to enforce civil rights and equal education laws despite political pressure not to. Mr. Panetta later practiced law in Monterey as a partner in Panetta, Thompson & Panetta from 1971 until 1976 when he was elected to Congress.

Mr. Panetta was a member of U.S. House of Representatives from 1976 until 1994. During his time in Congress, his work concentrated mostly on budget issues, civil rights, education, health, and environmental issues, particularly concentrating on preventing oil drilling off the California coastline. Mr. Panetta served as chairman of several committees including the U.S. House

Committee on the Budget, Agricultural Committee's Subcommittee on Domestic Marketing, Consumer Relations and Nutrition, and the Task Force on Domestic Hunger. He was also the vice-chairman of the Caucus of Vietnam-Era Veterans in Congress and a member of the President's Commission on Foreign League and International Studies. Mr. Panetta also authored the Hunger Prevention Act of 1988 and the Fair Employment Practices Resolution. In 1994 President Bill Clinton appointed him White House Chief of Staff, a position he served in until1996.

Mr. Panetta has served as a leader in numerous community and national public policy organizations throughout his career, including the Iraq Study Group and the Independent Task Force on Immigration and America's Future. In November 2004, California Governor Arnold Schwarzenegger appointed him co-chair of the Council on Base Support and Retention. He also served a six-year term on the Board of Directors of the New York Stock Exchange. Mr. Panetta currently serves as Distinguish Scholar to the Chancellor of the California State University system. He is also Presidential Professor of Santa Clara University, where he teaches a course on of public policy. He is the recipient of numerous awards including the 2006 Paul Peck Award, the 2003 Julius Stratton "Champion of the Coast" Award for Coastal Leadership, and the 1995 Distinguished Public Service Medal from the Center for the Study of the Presidency.

LARRY W. SONSINI is the Chairman and former CEO of Wilson, Sonsini, Goodrich & Rosati in Palo Alto, California. He attended the University of California, Berkeley where he earned his undergraduate in 1963 and his J.D. in 1966. He gained international recognition for his expertise in the areas of corporate law, corporate governance, securities regulation, and mergers and acquisitions.

Mr. Sonsini has been instrumental in many of the IPOs, mergers and acquisitions and other corporate transactions in Silicon Valley and beyond. He has represented some of Silicon Valley's most successful and renowned companies, including Google, Pixar, Apple, and Sun Microsystems. Some of the most well known transactions in which Mr. Sonini has participated as counsel include Google's historic IPO, Hewlett Packard's merger with Compaq Computer, and HP's formation of Agilent Technologies.

In addition to serving as Wilson Sonsini's CEO and Chairman for more than 20 years, Mr. Sonsini was also a member of the Board of Directors of the New York Stock Exchange from 2001 to 2003. Currently, he is the chairman of the NYSE's Regulation, Enforcement and Listing Standards Committee and is also chairman of its Legal Advisory Committee. In 2007 he was named One of the Most Influential Players in U.S. Corporate Governance by *Directorship* magazine and was named Business Leader of the Year by the Harvard Business School Association of Northern California in 2005. *Fortune* magazine also named Mr. Sonsini "the most influential and well-connected lawyer in the industry."

Mr. Sonsini has received multiple awards including the Business Hall of Fame Award from the Bay Area Council; the Community Service Award for Exemplary Leadership from the National Conference for Community and Justice; the Award for Achievement from the California Alumni Association of the University of California, Berkeley; the Special Achievement Award in Commerce and Law from the National Italian American Foundation; and an Honorary Doctorate from the Pacific Graduate School of Psychology. In 2004, he co-authored *Creating an Effective Board* for the Globe White Page Boardroom Advisor Series.

FOREWORD

Bob Cullen has got it right when he says that it's about time that "lawyers get in on the (leadership) game." None of us, lawyer or non-lawyer, has to settle for the viewpoint that you either are or are not a leader or, as Bob writes the idea that some people got it and others don't. Being a good lawyer and being a good leader are not mutually exclusive. The point is that high performance at an individual, organizational or even societal level requires leadership. Indeed, without leadership, progress is not possible. As management guru Peter Drucker is credited with saying: "Only three things happen naturally in organizations: frustration, confusion and under-performance. Everything else requires leadership."

Look up the word "leadership" in the dictionary, and see what it says: "to travel, to guide, to go." Leadership is all about taking people to places that they have never been before.[1] It is all about finding solutions to problems that have never existed before; and making the most of opportunities that are peeking out just beyond the horizon. To paraphrase Einstein: insanity is the belief that one can solve a problem by using the same tools or mind set which crafted that problem in the first place. We call upon lawyers and the legal profession to help us do things we have never done before; to make things happen which are not currently taking place; to address problems that are not taking care of themselves. Don't get me wrong, there is lots of room for disagreement about the best solution, but no denying the fact that none of us would be talking or taking any actions if someone or something hadn't stirred our imaginations to new possibilities (or at least a distinct unhappiness with the way things are right now).

Lawyers have not traditionally been educated for leadership, or at least not so directly, though history records the impact (leadership) that lawyers have had upon the world. And it's not just lawyers whose formal education experiences have typically been devoid of leadership development. The same can be said about medical practitioners, engineers, architects, scientists, teachers, politicians, civil servants, and even law enforcement personnel. Each profession, each guild and craft, has educated its members for competence – expertise in their subject matter – all too often at the expense of understanding what to do with that same expertise to frame a more just and humane enterprise, community or nation. As St. Ignatius of Loyola, founder of the Jesuit Order, who adopted education as the route to enabling a better world, explained: "To know and not to do, is not to know."

While Bob properly looks at the skills required for lawyers (and for that matter for the rest of us) to lead, let me underscore even more strongly the necessity of becoming a leader through exploration of your inner territory, for that's where action begins. You need to be asking yourself such questions as: Who am I? Why do I do what I do? What really matters? Who am I serving? What sacrifices am I willing to make, or not? There's too much attention being given to the head, and not enough to the heart.[2]

Leadership begins with the heart. Leaving all the jokes aside about the nature, or size, of a lawyer's heart, the truth of the matter for leaders in any realm or profession is that leadership begins with something that grabs hold of you and simply won't let go. Of course this sub-text reveals itself nicely in "principles" that are so well articulated by all of the *Leading Lawyers* that Bob interviewed and studied, and quotes (their wisdom) throughout this text. But if you are just picking up this book you've got to ask yourself, so where did Cabraser, Garza, Giuliani, Grey, Heineman, Kennard, Krupp, Loris, Panetta, Sonsini – or Marshall, Lincoln, Gardner, Klein, and the dozens of other examples provided by Bob get these "insights" in the first place? Read the life story Bob shares about Justice Kennard and you get the sense of how the person makes the lawyer and not the other way around.

I hope you use this wonderfully insightful and practical book that Bob has written to help you "find your voice" and to recognize the crucial cornerstone that "relationships" have in the leadership process. In every book on leadership, this one and any that I've co-authored, we can't tell you the words to say as a leader because then they would lack the authenticity required of leaders. This is similar to what author Anne Lamont tells would-be writers: You cannot write out of someone else's experiences. You have to write out of your own. Otherwise, the words sound like someone else rather than who you are and what you are about.

Certainly – whether as writers, lawyers, or as leaders – the leadership development process begins by learning about the techniques and mastering the tools of your craft, but this is simply the first stage in the process. In the second stage, you learn about the "masters" of your craft and determine what they did and attempt to copy or mimic their styles or try on their clothes in your attempt to become one of them. Many never progress beyond this stage to the final one which involves finding your own voice, your own style, your own answers to the questions of right-and-wrong, of what matters and what is trivial, of what to focus on and what not to be distracted by, of who and what in your life matters.

This final stage takes you deep within yourself, requires you to explore your inner territory (even those places that you may have locked away or find frightening), and eventually to locate your own true internal magnetic north.

But leadership is not just about you. It's about a relationship with others, and recognition that nothing extraordinary is accomplished all alone. Building such relationships as a leader will eventually mean putting the welfare of others above your own, for only in this manner will others want to make the commitments to you and to your voice that are eventually required for greatness: "I want to be in a relationship with you," (personally and/or organizationally), "because by doing so I will be better off than I would be by myself." And what sustains this relationship in the long run is recognizing and appreciating the paradox that leaders turn their followers into leaders themselves.

Finally, as Bob reminds us, while leadership is necessary for success, it is neither sufficient nor can it guarantee success. At a fundamental level, leadership is an act of faith, a belief in a better outcome or future. We've come full circle because leadership is a test of who we are and what we care about. Leadership author Patrick Lenconi told us that he learned early on that despite his earnest desires to lead before it could happen he had to wrestle with the fundamental questions of "Who did I want to serve?" and "Am I ready to sacrifice?"[3] If leadership were easy we would all be doing it, and books like Bob's and mine would be unnecessary. The fact is that leadership is hard work, the personal gains may be minimal, and the costs great.

But you (this reader, right now) are different, and you believe that you make a difference and that what you do matters, and that the law and your legal practice are a means to a better tomorrow. Bob and I salute you. Read on, and get ready to accept the challenge of taking us to places we've never been before.

Barry Z. Posner, PhD
Dean and Professor of Leadership
Santa Clara University

References:

1. James M. Kouzes and Barry Z. Posner. The Leadership Challenge, 4th Edition (SF: Jossey-Bass/Wiley Publishers, 2007).

2. James M. Kouzes and Barry Z. Posner. A Leader's Legacy (SF: Jossey-Bass/Wiley Publishers, 2006).

3. James M. Kouzes and Barry Z. Posner. *Christian Reflections on The Leadership Challenge* (SF: Jossey-Bass/Wiley Publishers, 2004).

Table of Contents

CHAPTER ONE:
The Stock Options Are
in Column B

After spending a few years teaching in the law school at Santa Clara University, I was hired by John Baird, a well-known leadership expert and principal in ExecutivEdge Consulting, a very high-level Silicon Valley executive leadership and coaching firm. Together, John and I, with another colleague, created a leadership seminar which was presented to the corporate legal department of a multibillion-dollar Silicon Valley software company.

We worked under the auspices of the company's senior vice president, who was troubled by complaints from department heads, indicating that their in-house lawyers considered themselves defenders of the corporate assets, risk avoiders, and did not adequately understand the needs, issues, or overall goals of the company's other departments. The lawyers were often criticized for getting in the way of innovative deals, they were not always the best team members, and they sometimes interfered with productive interdepartmental efforts. They were focused on risks to the company rather than problem-solving opportunities. This, as we all know, is not an atypical complaint; and, interestingly, the idea that an in-house lawyer is a protector of the corporate assets is a valid concept. However, the senior VP wanted the lawyers to become integrated team players, facilitate more deals, and help

"The purpose of leadership isn't to put money in your pocket or to acquire fame. The purpose of leadership is to improve the future. It's to improve the lives of others for the future."

Leon Panetta
Panetta Institute for
Public Policy

"Lawyers are taught to be very powerful analytically, but they are not always taught to ask large questions and then to understand what tools are necessary to answer those questions... My view of leadership is broad. It is not just "legal leadership," it is leadership in a variety of different settings, whether it is intellectual, non-profit, for-profit, executive branch or legislative leadership."

Ben Heineman, Jr.
Former General
Counsel for
General Electric

1

the company innovate responsibly, in addition to their traditional roles of ensuring appropriate risk-mitigating safeguards.

In a meeting with the senior vice president, we started listing conventional skills of lawyers (Column A) and outlining attributes on which the he wanted us to focus (Column B). These were our whiteboard lists:

COLUMN A	COLUMN B
Analytical	Innovative
Advocate	Collaborative
Detail-oriented	Goal-oriented
Law-driven	Team driven
Critical	Cooperative
Protective	Opportunity-oriented

As we were writing these descriptions, I knew that Column B skills were not natural to attorneys. I was concerned that our educational and professional tradition did not provide us with the appropriate background. Lawyers are trained to assess existing conditions and legal constraints and to minimize risk. We were trained by our law schools in the skills of Column A, not those of Column B. Most of our time was spent learning how to think like lawyers, advocating rights and positions, and reading appellate decisions and statutes. We generally are not trained to understand business models, develop business solutions, or facilitate new economic or social possibilities. After graduation, most of us spent our professional careers using Column A skills almost exclusively. During our brainstorming session, I wondered how the lawyers would be motivated to learn the Column B skills. I came to the conclusion that it would take innovative training and renewed motivation. However, what would be the incentive for lawyers to redirect their skill sets and integrate these qualities into their jobs and practices?

Then, the senior VP provided us with an insight into one's motivation for change. When I asked him about the incentives in the corporation for lawyers and their career paths in the business, he said that he hoped to make it clear to all of his employees, including the law department, that the stock options are in Column B. This remark came at a time when stock options were more popular in Silicon Valley, but his point was clear: lawyers who possess both legal and leadership skills had the best chance of career success in this billion-dollar software company. The VP expected all of the employees, including attorneys, to maintain their core skills and develop leadership skills. If one wanted to become general counsel, one needed to master the skills of Column B.

I came away from that experience thinking that the advocacy model, which focuses on the protection of rights and is the foundation of our legal education and practice, was not broad enough to deal with the varied roles that lawyers must fill in the New Economy. In this case, the VP wanted more from his lawyers: he wanted imaginative thinkers and team members. He needed them to provide top-level legal analysis and protect the assets of the corporation, but he also wanted them to build relationships with their clients and help meet corporate goals. Most of all, he wanted the lawyers to become business partners and leaders within the organization beyond their expertise in the law.

I would not suggest, of course, that we eliminate the traditional basis of our mission. Advocacy, reducing risk, and protecting rights and obligations are central components of our jobs in the criminal justice system, civil litigation setting, and in our practices in general. However, the advocacy and rights-protection model is inadequate to deal with many of our clients' concerns. In the business world, the government sector, and even service-based nonprofits, many lawyers find themselves in situations which are neither rights-driven nor advocacy-oriented. In the corporate setting, reduction of risk and protection of rights and assets is an important part of the overriding goal for general corporate counsel, but it is not enough. While we cannot eliminate the rights and advocacy model, our clients want us to simultaneously join in the collaboration process to solve problems and create positive change. In other words, lawyers need a new menu, where we pick one from Column A and have the ability to pick one from Column B. We need to become more diverse advocates to not just champion our client's position, but also generate creative solutions and initiate positive change.

1. Leadership Is the Essential Characteristic of a Successful Organization

Leadership skills are not some vague and amorphous idea (lawyers, stop rolling your eyes). We can all hone our abilities to become more persuasive and substantive experts; in addition, by learning a few simple concepts, we can become something more: we can become Leading Lawyers. Clients want, and are in fact beginning to demand, that you combine your lawyering talents with leadership skills. The need to develop and expand leadership qualities has for decades been religiously preached in widely respected and commonly used business and government leadership models across the globe. Why is it important? Because therein lies the future of the legal profession and the key to our success. Let me provide you with a few examples of how the exceptional use of leadership ability allowed individuals to create positive and lasting change within their organization.

The Best Businesses in the Nation Teach Leadership

One of the fundamental keys to Chairman and CEO Jack Welch's success at General Electric was his leadership insights and his *desire to teach* leadership techniques to General Electric employees. Welch devoted half of his time to "people" issues because he believed in the power and abilities of his people at GE. He connected with all levels of GE, from his top executives to the hourly worker. Welch was known to make random visits to GE's plants and offices, eat lunches with managers, and was famous for his personal handwritten notes to employees.[1] Employees felt as though Welch cared about them and their jobs, and the notes served to both inspire and demand action.

He was also a *dedicated* leader, continuously teaching three-week development courses throughout his career for different managerial levels; he chaired all strategic planning meetings with GE's top 500 executives in Boca Raton and also taught leadership sessions at Crotonville, a dedicated management training center. As a result, Welch's leadership style was replicated through the ranks, and "best practices" were shared among GE's differing businesses. Welch set specific performance goals and monitored them throughout the year in addition to giving his direct-reports written performance evaluations. Again, Welch's style of accountability was repeated by his business chiefs and their direct reports so that a cohesive system existed, and because "...the function of leadership is to produce more leaders, not more followers."[2] The business characteristics Welch implemented led to the development of leaders at all levels of GE and to GE's monumental success between 1981 and 2000.

Former Goldman Sachs CEO Henry Paulson (and current Secretary of Treasury), made it his practice to teach six-hour accountability and leadership sessions to all 1,200 of his managing directors while heading the world's largest investment bank. Paulson also made it a point to speak at the orientation for new analysts and associates. He evaluated the health of the company and planned for its future by discussing its successes as well as addressing his and Goldman Sachs' mistakes; he continually sought to learn from those mistakes and make improvements.[3] The culture of leadership is critical at Goldman

Sachs according to managing director John Rogers: "Our bankers travel on the same planes as our competitors. We stay in the same hotels. In a lot of cases, we have the same clients as our competition. So when it comes down to it, it is a combination of execution and culture that makes the difference between us and other firms."[4]

The pattern of CEO-level involvement in leadership development is also part of Best Buy's success. CEO Brad Anderson personally works with 100 to 200 Best Buy employees every month.[5] He focuses on this personal and an informal style of coaching because, in his opinion, it is more genuine and conducive to fostering a human connection.

Cisco Systems is run by John Chambers, who is interestingly enough a businessman *and* a lawyer. Chambers once said that:

> *Fifteen years ago we said we would change the way the world works, lives, plays and learns. Today, this company has the ability to understand and adapt to change, with a balance of leadership in four key customer segments. We have the courage to change, are setting the pace for change in our industry that's never been seen before, and have the vision to take our customers into the future...*[6]

At Cisco, leadership development has been made a key component to employee success. It is supported through e-learning classes and more traditional advanced degree programs. The e-learning classes were developed by Cisco to further the development of team leaders and managers.[7] Employees have the choice of instructor-led, Web-based, or e-tool courses which develop skills in the area of coaching, business, networking, management, and leadership. Cisco also offers employees the ability to obtain advanced degrees in business administration, engineering, and technology during the course of their employment.

It is easy to see that the common denominator to the success of these corporate giants is their fundamental understanding that leadership development is needed to maximize output from their employees and themselves. Whether it be through a personal note or an online tutorial, leadership training is an essential element to a successful organization.

The Best Professional Schools in the Nation Teach Leadership

The best professional schools also teach leadership as an important skill needed for educational success. Credible scholars have compiled reliable research on the attributes and skills that make a leader successful, and have produced sound leadership models that are academically grounded and, most important, functional. The two primary branches of research on leadership have developed in the business schools and universities that focus on government and public sector leadership and have become sources upon which we can rely.

Harvard, Stanford, Wharton, and many other business schools have been studying leadership in their organizational behavior departments for decades, and leading universities across the nation have strong leadership curricula for their business graduate students. At Santa Clara University, we are lucky to have one of the leading scholars in this area, Barry Posner. He is the coauthor of *The Leadership Challenge*, a seminal work on leadership in the business world. Naturally, the business school at Santa Clara places a strong emphasis on leadership as important to the overarching mission of the university.

The universities that focus on government and public policy issues, such as Harvard and Yale, conduct extensive studies on, and analysis of, leadership performance. No better work exists than that of Harvard's Kennedy School of Government, which has developed a variety of leadership classes. These schools have some of the best and brightest scholars evaluating leadership concepts at both the worldwide geopolitical and the local political levels. A look at their executive educational programs gives us just a small insight into the breadth of their studies. Their courses include: Leadership for a Networked World, providing a practical guide to the design of new governance and institutional structures for a heavily networked, boundary-crossing world; Innovations in Governance, which is an intensive executive education program designed to help lead changing organizations; Performance Measurement for Effective Management of Nonprofit Organizations, which is an intense executive education program designed for nonprofit leaders who want to improve the performance of their organizations; and Women and Power: Leadership in a New World, an intense, interactive experience designed to help women advance to top positions of influence in public leadership.[8]

Additionally, Stanford has a dedicated Center for Leadership Research and Development. Their curricula include courses on: Customer-Focused Innovation, describing how companies must create a culture of innovation that harnesses the creativity of its customers, users, and employees; Executive Program in Leadership: The Effective Use of Power, an executive program in leadership designed to help participants put effective, collaborative methods of leadership to work in their organizations and leverage the leadership potential of all members of their teams; and Interpersonal Dynamics for High-Performance Executives, discussing how business leaders live in an increasingly interdependent world where you need others to get your work done with a workshop focusing on improving your emotional intelligence.[9]

Furthermore, even though the primary sources for leadership literature are the schools of government and business, almost every professional graduate school is turning to leadership as a necessary complement to the specialty that it teaches. Even engineering and medical schools are teaching the importance of leadership as a desirable and even necessary component of their specialties. The Massachusetts Institute of Technology (MIT) has implemented a separate leadership class in its Engineering Systems Division called ESD.801: Leadership Development, last taught by Professor Dava Newman, who also teaches Aeronautics and Astronautics and Engineering Systems, is the Director of MIT's Technology and Policy Program, a MacVicar Faculty Fellow, and holds several prestigious degrees. In the manufacturing department, MIT has created the Leaders for Manufacturing Program dedicated to technical skills and leadership which is "the critical skill that embraces all other activities and gives them focus and direction."[10]

This brief overview of classes being offered at some of our nation's top universities is meant to illustrate the growing importance that scholars, public officials, and businesses in all areas are placing on leadership. However, as I am sure you have noticed, there were no examples of law schools that take the same approach to leadership development. That is because there are very few law schools that incorporate leadership skills courses into their curriculum. The best schools in government, health, engineering, and business make leadership a key component in their undergraduate, graduate, and executive educational curricula, but law schools remain behind the curve in that regard. Our leading scholars study leadership; our clients in government, business, and the nonprofit world study it: it is time we lawyers got in on the action.

7

2. In the New Economy, Leadership Is Imperative

The New Economy is a term that was coined in the 1990s to describe the evolution of the United States, and other developed countries, from an industrial/manufacturing-based economy to a knowledge/services-based economy. This shift arose partly due to the increased availability of, and drastic advancements in, technology and partly due to the effects of globalization.[11] It therefore should come as no surprise that our clients and their businesses have also shifted their focus to knowledge-based business models. As knowledge and expertise become more accessible, smaller businesses and firms find easier entrance into new markets. Businesses and firms must now rely on developing new skills sets, fresh management concepts, and innovative leadership ideas in order to operate at peak heights and remain competitive in this New Economy.

Carl J. Schramm is the president of one of America's largest foundations, the Kauffman Foundation, which operates nationwide to promote an entrepreneurial society in which job creation, innovation, and the economy flourish.[12] Schramm wrote in his book, *The Entrepreneurial Imperative*, that entrepreneurial capitalism is a unique resource in the business world that should be nurtured in its institutions. He outlines entrepreneurial capitalism as an economic and strategic pathway for the economy that rewards risk-taking by those who set out to be creative and innovative and who produce a product or service that generates wealth and jobs as well as security. He predicts that for the United States to survive and sustain its leadership role in the world, politically and economically, businesses must treat entrepreneurship as their central comparative advantage.[13]

The corollary for the legal profession is that *leadership* is the best model for our careers as individual lawyers and as members of organizations; leadership skills are essential for us to remain competitive in an entrepreneurial world. *If entrepreneurship is the business sector's imperative, then leadership is the imperative of the legal profession.* This applies to every sector of law including firms that provide services to their clients and participate in the community in which they work and live, legal departments that provide services to their corporate partners, nonprofits who serve the needs of their constituents, and governmental agencies that serve the public and their establishments. Leadership provides *the* advantage for lawyers and legal institutions. Exceptional legal knowledge and expertise are demanded by our clients, the courts, our organizations, and by society in general, but leadership skill sets and providing outstanding service beyond traditional legal analysis and advocacy is the new critical component to effective lawyering for entrepreneurial clients.

For the last 30 years, researchers have focused on identifying the key traits and skill sets common among the most successful leaders and as Shumeet Banerji, the CEO of Booz & Company, fully understands, "it is no longer good enough to offer advice. Clients want tangible outcomes with superior execution."[14] What skills then should lawyers have in order to provide their clients with those tangible results in the New Economy?

3. The Leadership Skills Needed in the New Eeconomy

Russell Palmer, the dean of the Wharton School of Business, and also a businessman with extensive experience as the CEO of several corporations, wrote in his book *Ultimate Leadership* that:

> *Leadership is the main differentiator in performance in most environments. People think that formulas, slick marketing, being first, the latest management tool, programs such as Six Sigma, and so on are the key differentiators in an organization. These other areas matter, but leadership alone is the key differentiator between organizations that succeed and those that fail.*[15]

In this new knowledge-based economy, and because information and experience have become more of a commodity, the critical success factors for businesses and professional service firms are leadership skills comprised of credibility, drive and determination, communication and persuasion, creative thinking, vision, and relationship and team building. Lawyers need these leadership skills in order to successfully navigate their clients through an ever-increasing sea of laws, regulations, and sophisticated business concepts in a way that separates themselves from their competition.

Credibility: Credibility is made of three prongs: expertise, integrity, and dynamism or inspiration. Clients expect that their lawyer will have the legal knowledge and expertise to provide necessary legal solutions; this is an area where lawyers have excelled and will continue to improve. Beyond law school a host of seminars, continuing legal education programs, and substantive in-house training seminars provide a basis for the education of our professionals. However, while subject matter expertise and experience will continue to be important, it proportionately diminishes in importance as firms, corporate legal departments, and practitioners of all backgrounds gain greater access to information. Therefore, lawyers must compete in areas other than just legal proficiency as expertise will become a threshold. Individual and institutional credibility also require characteristics of integrity and dynamism or inspiration as the basis of their credibility. Leading Lawyers that develop all three prongs of credibility will be the most competitive.

Drive and Determination: In this New Economy, it will be the lawyers who advocate the highest of standards and lead by their example that will experience the greatest satisfaction and success. Leading lawyers will seek responsibility and take the initiative to create positive change for their clients or organizations. Beyond all else, a leader understands the need for good old-fashioned hard work. They are ambitious but have the capacity to adapt to changing conditions. These successful lawyers are not only analytically and technically superior in their fields, but they seek to motivate and inspire others in order to further their leadership goals.

Innovation, Entrepreneurship, and Creative Problem-Solving: Lawyers will also have to become more innovative, forward-looking, creative, and cooperative as these skills are necessary to compete in the New Economy. Without forgetting our roles as the protector of our clients' rights, we can expand our roles to correspond to the characteristics this new economic system. The legal profession needs to engage its New Economy clients and provide solutions and opportunities that go beyond traditional advice. If we practicing lawyers only serve our clients in conformity with tradition, we fail to fully meet their evolving New Economy needs.

Communication and Persuasion: Leading Lawyers realize that there are many ways in which to communicate different messages to different people. They will identify the appropriate communication tool and use it in the most persuasive manner in order to implement their vision and accomplish positive change. Effective communication may require the recitation of cold hard facts in appeal to a rational audience or an illustrative analogy that appeals more to the emotions of the listener. The bottom line is that advocacy is not always the best method of communication for a lawyer to employ in the New Economy because clients are looking for deal makers and counselors, not deal breakers and naysayers.

Relationship Building. This is an area where Leading Lawyers excel beyond most others. They do not dismiss the emotional components of communication and persuasion and consistently show strong emotional character and integrity. People who are known to be honest, steady, and reliable often have a competitive edge and their relationships are deep and well-established. It is a primary goal of Leading Lawyers to develop relationships, motivate others, and build well-working teams in every environment. Even in highly stressful situations such as litigation, they establish a working relationship whenever possible, including with their clients and even with opposing counsel and parties. They take a collaborative, noncompetitive approach to many situations, are good at listening, and are open to new ideas. Leading Lawyers use a variety of information-gathering techniques to gather vital information through conversation, dialogue, questions, and interaction. They thoroughly vet their ideas with their colleagues, learn from their adversaries, and collaborate whenever possible. Through inquiry and collaboration, they develop their own emotional insights and inspire the same awareness and capacities in their team members.

All of the skill sets listed above can be learned, and should be cultivated, through leadership development programs within the legal organization. Leadership development and training is the primary element for a competitive future in the legal community. Lawyers will continue to expand their breadth of legal expertise and efficiency through technology advancements, but lawyers will need creative economic approaches and expansive skills (beyond our traditional advocacy and research-based set) to identify needs, opportunities, and solutions for our clients. We need to learn the skills not typically taught in our law school education: how to communicate with and develop a better understanding of our clients; to approach problems collaboratively and creatively, rather than with a solely adversarial approach; to work well with our associates, peers, and even our adversaries; to utilize teams efficiently and productively; to bring the human element (emotions, motivation, and culture) into a discipline that is notoriously suspicious of anything it sees as irrational, emotional, or unquantifiable.

Law firms, legal organizations, and corporations compete by attracting and developing the most promising attorneys and shaping them into the finest lawyers *and* leaders. Human capital and leadership talent is the distinguishing factor for success now and in the future. On an individual basis, development of leadership skills is an unequivocal way to improve one's career path and direction. "Any firm that can outperform its competition in building and creating skills, will gain a significant advantage…Competitive advantage does not come from an ability to hire better people than your competitors, but from a superior ability to develop them."[16]

Notes

1. John A. Byrne, "How Jack Welch Runs GE", BusinessWeek, 3-4, (June 8, 1998).

2. Ralph Nader, http://www.wisdomquotes.com/cat leadership.html (accessed September 4, 2008).

3. Christopher Tkaczyk, "Follow These Leaders", Fortune, (Dec. 12, 2005).

4. Harvard Business School Case Study, Leadership Development at Goldman Sachs, #9-405-002, (February 23, 2006).

5. Tkaczyk, *supra* note 3.

6. http://tools.cisco.com/dlls/tln/page/executives/chambers (accessed May 24, 2008).

7. http://www.cisco.com/web/about/ac227/about cisco corp citi faqs.html (accessed May 24, 2008).

8. Harvard Executive Leadership Guide, (2005-2006), http://content.ksg.harvard.edu/leadership/index.php?option=com content&task=view&id=6&Itemid=14.

9. Stanford Leadership Center for Leadership Research and Development, Organizational Leadership Courses, (2005- 2006), http://www.gsb.stanford.edu/cldr/teaching/courses.html.

10. http://lfm.mit.edu/curriculum.html (accessed May 27, 2008).

11. http://en.wikipedia.org/wiki/New economy (accessed July 2007).

12. http://www.kauffman.org/foundation.cfm (accessed July 2007).

13. Carl J. Schramm, *The Entrepreneurial Imperative*, 1 Collins Publishers (2006).

14. Strategy&Business, Summer 2008 edition, *available at* http://www.strategy-business.com/search/archives/?issue=26906650.

15. Russell E. Palmer, *Ultimate Leadership*, 11 Wharton School Publishing (2008).

16. David Maister, *True Professionalism*, 105 Free Press (1997).

CHAPTER TWO:
Leadership Roles for Lawyers

1. Leadership for Lawyers

A significant problem for lawyers who want to become leaders is deciphering the unusually complex array of ideas, definitions, and models in what seems to be an immeasurable amount of leadership material. Lawyers must navigate through the literature and read about the applicability of leadership skills in many different arenas. Also, although many of the leadership books available can be entertaining, a majority of them are nondescript and frankly, not helpful to gaining a useful understanding of what skills makes a Leading Lawyer successful or how to cultivate those necessary skills. So where do lawyers turn to in order to learn how to be effective leaders in a legal context? We turn to credible, academic, and well-established research that will help us cut through the marketing concepts of existing leadership literature and apply those concepts in the legal arena, in addition to evaluating the experience, insights, and successes of lawyers who are already Leading Lawyers. In doing just that, we have developed a definition of leadership at Santa Clara University School of Law; leadership for lawyers is *"[t]he process by which an individual or group influences others to achieve positive, ethical change."*[1]

The dean of Santa Clara's School of Law, Donald Polden, makes several important points about the elements of our definition of leadership. First, leadership is a <u>process</u>; it is

"As a lawyer, you're getting a license, not only to practice law; you're getting a license to be a leader."

Leon Panetta
Panetta Institute for
Public Policy

"Lawyers can play and serve many different roles and they can do it at the same time. They can be an advisor, while being a counselor and problem-solver, while being an advocate. If that person is a very special person, they can wear all these hats at various times."

Robert Grey
Former President of
the American Bar
Association

13

not just a position.[2] Some people are put in leadership positions, but the position itself does not solely define the leader. Rather, the position merely gives the individual a leadership opportunity. People in leadership positions may or may not be good leaders. Leaders *emerge* in organizations and situations where they are called upon to create change and they continually rely upon their skills, relationships, and insights as a process.

Second, leadership requires influence.[3] Again, there are different ways to communicate with others and persuade them that change is necessary. Advocacy may be the appropriate way to persuade in one circumstance or situation, yet it might not work in another. When it will be more effective, Leading Lawyers move from advocacy to supportive and constructive communication, negotiation, and conflict resolution. Also, they lead and persuade by example by performing to the best of their ability.[4] Like California Supreme Court Justice Joyce Kennard said, "do the job that [you] have to the very best of [your] ability and to perform that job in a manner that shows integrity and independence."[5]

Third, practicing leadership requires the framing and creation of a vision or a solution that results in positive and ethical change.[6] This is a very important aspect of the leadership definition for the legal profession. This ethical and moral component is crucial to our professional obligations.

A fourth important point to keep in mind is that leadership is for everyone.[7] It is everyone's responsibility to learn and develop basic leadership skills[8] in order to advance the goals of your client and organization and the legal profession as a whole. We can become leaders by focusing on the skill sets common to successful Leading Lawyers and by incorporating those practices into our daily activities.

The credible evidence suggests that leadership is the essential ingredient to an extraordinary career in law. Lawyers use their legal knowledge and analytical expertise, but the most successful lawyers, the Leading Lawyers, go beyond these traditional lawyering skill sets. The research and interviews confirms that many lawyers are analytical and fine advocates, but Leading Lawyers are also innovative and wise counselors. Our clients are calling for more than advocacy and analysis; they want problems-solvers, integrators, creative-thinkers, team members, and team leaders. A Leading Lawyer challenges the status quo, has vision, and helps to initiate positive change through collaboration, determination, and persuasion, in addition to using the traditional advocacy model.

2. Leadership Is for Everyone

When talking about leadership, many commentators concentrate on the issues facing those at the top of an organization, such as the general counsel, the managing partner, and the department head. This is certainly one area to place emphasis on, but it is essential to examine leadership issues at every level of the organization and to ensure that all lawyers learn the skills of leadership. The most progressive organizations disseminate their views of leadership at all levels.

The need for leadership at all levels applies in most situations and events in life. One of my favorite sporting events is the Tour de France, which millions of people from all over the world watch every July. In 1981, when I first saw the Tour in Paris, one or two Americans participated in the event as support riders for European teams. We Americans on the Champs Elysees cheered for them wildly. That year, the great Bernard Hinault of France won the coveted Yellow Jersey. Since then, American Greg Lemond won the race three times and, of course, Lance Armstrong captured the world's attention with seven consecutive victories. The Tour provides a good analogy for why leadership is for everyone. Armstrong once described his team as it rode through the mountains:

> Frankie, George, Christian, Kevin and Peter worked the hardest. Frankie would start the rolling climbs, setting a strong tempo and dropping riders. When Frankie got tired, George would pull, and a few more riders would drop by the way side, unable to keep our pace. Then came Tyler, who would pick up the pace, dropping even more of our competitors. Finally, I would be left with Kevin, pulling me through the steeps.[9]

Every member of a legal team, like the cycling team, pulls and leads at some point.

As Kouzes and Posner remind us in their book, *The Leadership Challenge*, "[o]rdinary people [get] extraordinary things done…men and women, young and old, from a variety of organizations, public and private, government and third-sector, high-tech and low-tech, small and large, schools and professional services. Chances are you haven't heard of most of them. They're people who might live next door or work in the next cubicle over."[10] Kouzes and Posner

15

focused their research on everyday leaders because they firmly believe that leadership is not about position or title. In an interview with author Stephanie West Allen, Irene Sander discussed how the networks and hierarchies within a firm or organization make leadership important at all levels:

> [T]he concepts of leader and leadership need to be re-viewed through the lens of complexity, and currently there's a lot of discussion in the management literature about this subject. The term "leader" usually refers to a role or function within an organizational hierarchy, and the word "leadership" usually describes a set of behaviors or attributes demonstrated by the person or persons in the leader roles. But if we think of a complex adaptive human system as a network of self-organizing hubs of activity, then you see that leaders emerge depending on the activity and then dissipate or change when the activity is completed or changes.

> So it's important that everyone develop the attributes of leadership in order to take the lead should the need arise. Think for a minute about the elegant and changeable patterns created by a flock of birds. Leadership in the flock changes quickly depending on environmental conditions, yet there remains a discernible pattern to their movement together. In the structure of a law firm the partners are usually at the top of the hierarchy, but in practice there are many leaders at work in the administrative and case-related hubs of activity. So when I think about what this would look like on paper, I see a hybrid; a hierarchy alive with self-organizing tornadoes of activity.[11]

It's about relationships, credibility, and what you *do*. Beyond the practices, beyond the action steps, there is a fundamental truth about leadership: *leadership is everyone's business.*[12]

In the everyday battle of lawyering (and we all know it can feel like a battle sometimes), legal working groups face a multiplicity of issues and responsibilities. Everyone in an organization contributes as a team leader at some point.

As a litigator, I relied on a team of people to accomplish the numerous tasks involved. My paralegals worked with clients to answer interrogatories, respond to document requests, and many other aspects of discovery and trial preparation, in a timely fashion. I often handled sizable multiparty construction cases, and my assistant was charged with coordinating the schedule of large meetings with many lawyers, clients, and experts. In large settlement conferences where I was the lead attorney, we would often have to negotiate with as many as 50 parties. I put together negotiation teams with my associates, who would all be responsible at some point for developing the facts, laws, expert opinions, and negotiation points for each codefendant and then for negotiating a settlement with that party. Effective leadership and effective teamwork were essential in coordinating every part of these cases. Every member of the legal team leads in one way or another. The critical point is that leadership is for everyone.

This means that law organizations should focus their training as much on associates, junior partners, and administrators as they do on the managing partner or general counsel. Lawyers, with increasing frequency and more than members of any other profession, are called upon to sit on nonprofit boards, lead commissions, and provide leadership in the community. Because there has been a recent flurry of interest in intellectual capital, law schools, and law firms—as well as our legal departments and organizations—teaching the skills of creativity, relationship building, communication, and persuasion, will be more intensified. Dean Polden agrees. He wrote that leadership "is everyone's responsibility to consider and acquire basic leadership skills...[W]e develop our students by teaching *skills* in the law school's leadership programs. Like leadership education programs and courses in business schools, we focus on the skills necessary to develop our students into leaders through the articulation and identification of a set of skills and practices that are available to all lawyers."[13]

3. Small "l" Leadership and Big "L" Leadership

It is often difficult for people to grasp the concept that leadership is for everyone. How can a 200-person organization have 200 leaders? However, there are a host of different leadership opportunities within any organization; the organizations that train their employees in leadership skills will be the most successful. Cooperation, team work, understanding institutional goals and leadership skills at all levels is the key to a high-performance organization.

We all understand that a corporation has a CEO, the legal department has general counsel, and a law firm has a managing partner. We task those people with the role of Big "L" Leadership. These leaders need to have the highest level of expertise, credibility, vision, team implementation, and are responsible for upholding standards and policies in addition to all of the other tasks we expect of such positions. However, there are other supporting roles to be played. For example, the managing partner pushes down leadership responsibilities to department heads, and department heads disperse work throughout the group. When there is a new case, a new firm initiative, or a pro bono project, responsibility and leadership opportunities should be pushed downward. These smaller tasks that require implementation on the organizational and team level, that will ultimately translate into the success (or failure) of a project, are what I call small "l" leadership opportunities.

Jeffrey Lutsky, managing partner of Stradley, Ronon, Stevens & Young, once said that one of the most common complaints from managing partners in large law firms is a perceived lack of future leaders within their firms.[14] In order to overcome this issue, we must create and seek more opportunities for small "l" leadership. We must train our law students, associates, and colleagues to recognize these leadership opportunities as they arise and accept them with an eye toward positive change. One does not typically start out as the CEO or GC; everyone needs to take on leadership responsibilities and they have to start out with small "l" leadership.

In so many situations, a senior lawyer will assign a junior lawyer a case having already provided the course of action with little or no input from the junior associate. A small "l" leadership opportunity is presented when the junior lawyer is introduced to the client earlier in the process, is allowed to participate and formulate an approach to solving the problem, or provides advice to improve the client's goals. Less-experienced lawyers that take on greater responsibility early in their career will be better equipped to handle these situations in the future.

For example, when Rudy Giuliani was the U.S. Attorney in charge of the Southern District of New York, he made it a priority to give his assistant U.S. Attorneys experience in small "l" leadership in order to better prepare them to take advantage of future Big "L" Leadership opportunities.[15] Mayor Koch and many of the state and federal drug agencies took note of significant drug activity on the lower east side of New York: what Giuliani described as an open-air drug market. As a Leading Lawyer, Giuliani recognized in the grave situation a chance to create positive change by cleaning up the street corners through the prosecution of more mid- to low-level drug offenders, and the chance to provide meaningful professional experience to his junior attorney's by allowing them to fully handle, and in many cases try, these drug prosecutions. His plan allowed his junior lawyers to gain much needed hands-on experience, provided them valuable trial work, and also helped to drastically reduce a dangerous societal problem. Importantly, Giuliani addressed these two needs by pushing down responsibility through the ranks and creating small "l" leadership opportunities for even the newest of attorneys.

Leading Lawyers promote skills, inquiry, and leadership from the top down. They encourage their junior lawyers to be innovative, build relationships with clients and colleagues, and creatively search for other problems and issues when a single dispute arises. Senior Leading Lawyers can better encourage junior lawyers by providing them with support and insight and allowing them to take responsibility: to contribute not just to limited areas, such as document review and research, but planning strategy, brainstorming, evaluating options, communicating with the client, and tracking outcomes. Junior Leading Lawyers can seek out these opportunities by engaging with senior lawyers and proactively seeking more responsibility at earlier stages in the process.

New lawyers should look for small "l" leadership opportunities and senior lawyers should provide those opportunities when available. It is only through a consistent and conscious choice to be a leader that one will become aware of greater opportunities and achieve positive and ethical change. Law organizations should work to create and train their members in leadership because it will be more successful and productive when it pushes down the idea of responsibility and leadership opportunities throughout the ranks. Ordinary people are capable of extraordinary things after they have learned to perform on small "l" leadership projects.

4. The Roles of Leading Lawyers

In today's competitive market, clients increasingly demand that lawyers serve not only as advocates and legal advisors, but as innovative business partners, counselors, and leaders. Moving beyond the role of situational or transaction-specific advisor, lawyers must be futurists and visionaries—they must discern trends in the law and predict how those trends will impact the company's business over time and alert managers so that plans can be designed to avoid pitfalls. Lawyers who develop the skills and flexibility to become analytical *and* creative—providing advice that not only protects their clients' legal interests, but also achieves their future goals—can help create opportunities in a wide variety of industries. Strategic Leading Lawyers move back and forth between these roles as appropriate circumstances arise.

	Advocate	Creative Problem Solver	Leading Lawyer
Evaluation	Evaluates the legal consequences of an issue.	Facilitates and develops a legal and business solution to the current problem.	Provides legal solutions, helps to create and define organizational opportunity and change.
Concerns	Concerned with legal issues and positions.	Concerned with legal issues, individual and business interests, and develops good working relationships.	Concerned with legal interests, business relationships, and organizational opportunities and change.
Priorities	Legal analysis is a priority.	Individual, group and business problems are equally important.	Opportunity, long-term improvement, legal and entrepreneurial business success are key issues.
Style	Assertive and direct, competitive, and sometimes adversarial.	Analytical, cooperative, creative, and facilitative.	Innovative, entrepreneurial, has creativity and long-term vision.
Client Interaction	Performs analysis and communicates conclusion.	Investigates, questions, listens, and consults.	Develops legal ideas along with organizational improvement, innovates, leads.
Process	Distributive process —zero sum game —divides the pie.	Integrative process— expanding the pie.	Process that creates value—expands the pie or develops a new pie; innovates with the client to solve immediate and foreseeable problems; improves organizational opportunity and efficiency.

When acting in their traditional roles as *advocates*, attorneys evaluate the legal consequences of an issue and act to advance the legal interests of their clients. The advocate's goal is to perform legal analysis, evaluate the options, and provide a conclusion. In litigation, the advocate typically employs this position-based skill set, sometimes in an aggressive, competitive, and adversarial manner. This is our traditional role. Some lawyers also rely on this model in business negotiations, especially when the need for a long-term relationship between the parties is not an issue. However, competitive negotiations and inflexible position-based advocacy is not always the best approach, such as when dealing with a client's long-term or potential business partner or when interacting with a corporate client's managers or board of directors. Problem solving should be the focus in most business settings. Innovative lawyers recognize that not all problems require legal solutions, and not all legal problems require advocacy.

To address both legal and business interests, the *problem-solving* lawyer, using a variety of skills, weighs the short- and long-term consequences, takes into consideration extra-legal issues, and works to facilitate a solution that strengthens the working relationships among the parties. No longer functioning only as an advocate, the attorney orchestrates and orders relationships within a legally and financially viable framework for the benefit of all involved, focusing on legal positions and solutions to assist the business prospects of the client. This approach requires a broader understanding of the client's problems and a wider investigation into potential solutions than attorneys who are in advocacy-mode generally undertake. Also, it begins the process of understanding the full leadership position that we sometimes are asked to perform.

There is a host of literature available on problem-solving models and methods; the key lies in the lawyer's ability to shift from issue identification, legal analysis, and conclusion to an open-minded investigation of the problem, a broad multi-disciplinary understanding, and creative analysis of the available legal and business solutions. While attorneys must refrain from acting solely as advocates when they should function as problem-solvers, they must also recognize that corporate clients often want them to go one step further and assist them in capturing opportunity and achieving their institutional goals.

The business world has always rewarded executives who move beyond solving an immediate problem and address the problem's roots in order to improve the organization. In our new economy, an entrepreneurial lawyer has become more valuable as well. Lawyers must therefore develop their ability to achieve legal solutions that fit the overall goals of the client and, when giving advice, *help to identify positive opportunities for change*. Lawyers who can move into this third, innovative, and nontraditional role—that of a Leading Lawyer—will see their business increase as they become more valuable to their clients.

When serving as an advisor to their client, the *Leading Lawyer* considers all contingencies and aspects of a situation when solving an immediate problem or suggesting changes to avoid future difficulties, including vendor relationships, market conditions, interdepartmental priorities, and business opportunities. He or she might even gather a team of multi-disciplinary professionals to deal with an organization's goals and needs. Then, with an eye on the client's existing and projected legal interests and business relationships, the Leading Lawyer proactively brainstorms with others. They will participate in interdisciplinary meetings that involve various departments such as engineering, marketing, or human resources, to identify areas for improvement before problems arise, recognize avenues of opportunity, and create value for the company or stakeholders whenever possible.

The Leading Lawyer offers new, dynamic ideas that not only advance the clients' business processes and goals, but also assists all players or principals involved. Such innovative lawyering not only benefits the client, but also the legal profession. Lawyers can, and will, come to be seen as partners who provide better solutions than the ones initially proposed, rather than cost centers who often say "no" to proposed actions. The three roles of advocate, creative problem solver, and Leading Lawyer are in fact closely intertwined and a successful lawyer will master all three. To place in context how a lawyer can be called upon to fulfill these roles, consider these examples involving intellectual property law.

As all lawyers are abundantly aware, clients can reap benefits from advice grounded in advocacy. As a recent example, Research in Motion (RIM), the Canadian maker of Blackberry was sued for infringement by NTP, Inc., a patent holding company. NTP alleged that RIM was infringing a number of its patents. In an epic litigation that almost found its way to the Supreme Court, RIM came dangerously close to having its entire U.S. network shut down under an injunctive order, only to be saved by the public policy considerations, pressed by the Department of Defense, pointing to the overwhelming reliance on the RIM device by law enforcement and first responders. The case eventually culminated in a settlement that cost RIM over $600 million. Without opining on foreseeability of such turbulent events, the lesson learned is the need for a lawyer to always practice an element of advocacy in advising his clients, evaluating perspective risks and positions. There is no doubt that NTP benefited from a strong advocacy-oriented approach to this litigation.

Furthermore, a creative problem-solving approach is useful in a situation where a client presents you with their company's "crown jewel" idea or concept. A patent may be a poor avenue of protection if the invention is difficult to replicate because a patent must contain full disclosure of the invention and will enable anyone to practice the invention upon its expiration. Recognizing that the client may lose protection earlier than was necessary if they patent their process, a creative problem-solving lawyer might actually advise their client against filing for a patent. Indeed, had Coca-Cola Co. been advised to patent its formula, it would have been public knowledge early in the 20th century. The creative advice to take careful measures to preserve confidentiality enabled Coca-Cola to avail itself of the benefits of trade secret laws instead of patent protection. The formula has been protected indefinitely as long as the requirements for trade secret protection continue to be met. By carefully guarding its formula, Coca-Cola is still reaping the rewards from their lawyer's creative problem-solving approach, and we are still enjoying the familiar taste that generations have grown to recognize from its original maker.

Another high-tech dispute will illustrate how a Leading Lawyer approaches a problem. Qualcomm, a key player in telecommunications, and Nokia, a renowned handset manufacturer, have been involved in a lengthy dispute over a number of patents held by the giants involving current and next generation telecom technology. In the summer of 2008, they entered into a 15-year deal, these giants reached a settlement, agreeing to cross-license a number of patents to one another. While the details remain confidential, the agreement is expected to facilitate further innovation in the telecom market as we head into the next generation of mobile telecommunications. This is the ultimate example of Leading Lawyers employing the key characteristics of advocacy, problem solving, and leadership through a complex dispute and negotiation, expanding the pie and enabling the parties to walk away with a relationship expected to yield a net positive sum, promoting further innovation in the marketplace.

The birth to dispute life of technology we just considered underscores the call upon lawyers to assist in developing a client's business strategies. The most sought-after lawyers are those who not only help organizations conform to existing regulations (e.g., simply procuring a patent), but also help identify advantageous relationships and growth opportunities. More and more clients are seeking out lawyers who seamlessly use these diverse skills to take on multiple roles.

5. Leadership Is Learned

We cannot discuss leadership without asking the question on everyone's mind: can people develop leadership skills? Are leaders made or born? It would be fair to say that everyone who writes on this subject and analyzes the evidence agrees: *leadership skills are learned; leaders are made, not born.* A perfect example is that of the U.S. Marine Corps, which has been developing leaders for well over 200 years. Its entire training model is based on making sure that all of its officers become leaders.

In their excellent book, *The Extraordinary Leaders*, John H. Zenger and Joseph Folkman research many aspects of leadership and assess many organizations. They examined the leadership development program of the U.S. Marine Corps and were so convinced of their findings that they declared: "We attest that leaders are made. While this is certainly not a new point of view; we go on record declaring this to be a fact."[16]

Zenger and Folkman thoroughly investigated the process the Marines use and noted that the Marines spend a significant amount of time developing their officers. The Marines send officers to a 10-week program of development to receive theoretical as well as practical information about leadership, and to participate in a variety of skill-building activities. Leaders are encouraged to find their natural talents and are not forced into unnatural molds. Rather than being rigid, the Marines understand that there are a variety of ways to lead. Some recruits are good technically, some are team builders, and some have a high level of organizational skills. The Marines emphasize helping potential officers to find their own voices and magnify their natural tendencies. They use highly engaging learning methods. The program involves planning under pressure; developing three detailed plans for each mission and choosing the best one; and carrying out missions. One of the best techniques is the "after action review," where a discussion and learning session take place after the mission. The trainers, experienced Marines, also relate personal stories of past missions. They use leadership books and manuals. The Marines collate approximately 100 books and manuals, which are taught seriously, and form a prescribed reading list. They provide cross-training outside one's area of expertise. Lawyers are assigned to command infantry units, while an infantry commander is transferred to head up a supply unit. All of these techniques allow recruits to *learn* how to become leaders. Lawyers might learn from the Marines how to emphasize collaboration, teamwork, and leadership at all levels.

Whether one is undertaking a 10-week Marine training course, a three-year law program, or simply reading a book on leadership, the goal is to understand and develop the skills of leadership. For attorneys, skills will supplement the analytical and advocacy talents that we gained in law school and hone as practitioners. Admittedly, some people have a natural tendency toward leadership, but those who do not can learn the skills necessary to be a leader. Developing credibility is the first step to becoming a Leading Lawyer.

Notes

[1.] Donald Polden, "Educating Law Students for Leadership Roles and Responsibilities", 39 U. Tol. L. Rev. 353, 355 (Winter 2008).

[2.] *Id.* at 355.

[3.] *Id.*

[4.] *Id.*

[5.] Interview with Justice Joyce Kennard, August 2008.

[6.] Polden, *supra* note 1.

[7.] James S. Kouzes & Barry Z. Posner, *The Leadership Challenge*, 337 Jossey-Bass, (4th ed. 2007).

[8.] Polden, *supra* note 1 at 104.

[9.] Lance Armstrong, *It's Not About the Bike: My Journey Back to Life*, 243 Berkeley Publishing Group (2001).

[10.] Kouzes and Posner, *supra* note 7 at 383.

[11.] http://westallen.typepad.com/idealawg/ (accessed August 2007).

[12.] Kouzes and Posner, *supra* note 10.

[13.] Polden, *supra* note 1 at 356.

[14.] Gina Pasarella, "Leadership Programs Born from Lack of Born Leaders", *Law.com* (November 16, 2007), *available at,* http://www.law.com/jsp/llf/PubArticleLLF.jsp?id=1195121055535.

[15.] Interview with Rudolf Guiliani, August 2008.

[16.] John H. Zenger and Joseph Folkman, *The Extraordinary Leaders*, 27 McGraw Hill (2002)

CHAPTER THREE:
Establish Credibility

Credibility is the foundation of leadership[1] and of our professional lives. Nothing is more important to the success of our careers and to the representation of our clients than our credibility as lawyers. Given the governmental, financial, and legal scandals of the last 20 years, this proviso is more applicable now than ever. We, as a profession, must continue to elevate our notions of ethics, morality, honesty, character, and personal discipline to the highest levels. However, what does this mean for the practicing attorney? Credibility and good reputation are both a goal and a process; each is earned, case by case, deal by deal, and relationship by relationship. It must be carefully maintained because once lost, credibility is not easily regained. Importantly, credibility can be earned through a dedication to honesty, inspiration, and substantive expertise. In looking around at the members of our profession, we all recognize the best lawyers and judges. How have they earned our respect? What are the skills and traits that define their credibility? Can we learn to be better and more credible lawyers and leaders ourselves? Credibility is something that is essential for a professional and can be improved, enhanced, and developed through deliberate and conscientious efforts.

1. Credibility Research

A person is credible when he is believable and convincing.[2] When a lawyer's expertise is recognized, their word can be trusted, their actions are consistent with their words, and they continually provide inspired solutions, they

> "When I think about the people I most admire, and what people say about them, there is always a reference to their integrity. That comes from being honest, consistent and always being respectful in dealing with others. It's also their intellects; they are impressive and they are experts. They have a professionalism and commitment to their profession and it is obvious that they care about their performance."
>
> **Deborah Garza**
> Deputy Assistant Attorney General for U.S. Department of Justice

> "Credibility is the gold standard in lawyering; the gold standard in litigation."
>
> **Elizabeth Cabraser**
> Lieff, Cabraser, Heimann & Bernstein, LLP

then possess the credibility for which we all strive. These themes are well-established in the available legal and leadership literature. They are exemplified in the stories told throughout this text and should be experienced in our everyday practice of law.

The scholarly examination of the idea of credibility is as old as the discussion of rhetoric itself, having originated with the ancient Greeks. As a practical matter, credibility is essential to our roles as lawyers:

> *General Counsel needs credibility and guts—in addition to legal skills and business acumen—when they are playing the role of the guardian of the company's integrity and reputation... Credibility comes, in part, from a GC's character, experience, reputation, self-confidence, and the ability to explain issues forcefully, clearly and concisely.*[3]

While plenty of anecdotal information on this subject is available, the ultimate test of these ideas is found in research performed by well-known leadership academics such as Kouzas and Posner in *The Leadership Challenge*[4] and Warren Bennis in *Leading for a Lifetime.*[5] Additional insight is gleaned from research performed in the communications world on what experts refer to as "source credibility." The results of the research in these areas are remarkably similar: to be credible, one must inspire trust and be an expert in their field. Below is a chart which shows the elements of credibility as outlined by the three sources of information that we examine.

CHARACTERISTICS OF CREDIBILITY					
	Honesty	Expertise	Dynamic	Visionary	Ambitious
Leadership Challenge	Honest	Competent	Inspiring	Forward-Looking	
Leading for a Lifetime	Moral Compass	Competent			Ambitious
Source Credibility– Academic Business Literature	Inspire Trust-	Expertise	Dynamic		

To provide you with the most well-researched and well-received information on what makes a person credible, I will focus on the leadership research of Kouzes and Posner, Warren Bennis, and literature from the academic business world.

a. The Leadership Challenge[6]

Through their research, and as explained in their book *The Leadership Challenge,* Kouzes and Posner have discovered that, "when they are performing at their best, leaders are doing more than just getting results. They're also responding to the expectations of their constituents..."[7] Kouzes and Posner have administered a questionnaire to over 75,000 people all over the globe in an effort to determine what traits people most admire in a leader and the results have been consistent across different cultures and demographics. The four most often cited characteristics of good leaders have time after time been: **Honesty, Forward-Looking, Competent,** and **Inspiring.** It is easy to see how these characteristics relate to our profession. We admire the lawyers who operate within a moral and ethical code and respect those who are experts in their fields. We respect lawyers who do what they say they will do and whose actions are consistent with their words. "[M]ore than anything, people want leaders who are credible."[8] After countless surveys, Kouzes and Posner conclude that credibility is the foundation of leadership and that honesty, vision, competence, and inspiration is what makes a leader credible. Those who aspire to be leaders in the legal profession, or otherwise, will seek to obtain and enhance these qualities.

Kouzes and Posner assert that no matter what the setting, everyone wants to be fully confident in their leaders, and to be fully confident they have to believe that their leaders are people of strong character and solid integrity; they have to believe their leader is **honest.**[9] If you practice what you preach, your constituents will be more willing to entrust in you their future.[10]

The Leadership Challenge also shows that more than 70% of their most recent survey respondents listed the **ability to look ahead** as one of the most sought-after traits in a leader. "People expect leaders to have a sense of direction and a concern for the future of the organization."[11] Leaders keep an eye to the future and seek opportunity for organizational change.

Furthermore, Kouzes and Posner's research shows that before someone will enlist in your vision, they must believe that the person is **competent** to guide them to where they are headed. People must see their leader as capable and effective. Kouzes and Posner emphasize that leadership "competence" refers to the leader's track record and ability to get things done. A leader must consistently demonstrate their ability to create positive change and a willingness to learn from their mistakes.

Lastly, their survey revealed that people expect their leaders to be **inspirational,** energetic, and positive about the future. Whatever the circumstances, when leaders breathe life into their aspirations, people are more willing to enlist in the movement.[12] Enthusiasm and excitement are essential because they signal your personal commitment to pursuing a dream.[13]

If successful in gaining the necessary credibility to occupy a role of leadership, as well as that of a successful lawyer, then you can influence clients and constituents and create organizational loyalty. In an extensive study performed by Fredrick Reichheld and his Bain & Company colleagues, he discovered that "businesses concentrating on customer, employee, and investor loyalty generate superior results…"[14] It logically follows that a lawyer who has the credibility to foster client, constituent, and organizational loyalty will also have an enhanced capacity to persuade and accomplish his goals and those of his clients. However, in many circumstances, credibility is one of the hardest attributes to earn and sustain[15] so leaders must never take credibility for granted, regardless of the times or their positions of authority.

b. Leading for a Lifetime[16]

Warren Bennis is another one of the leading experts in the United States on the subject of leadership. He has written 27 books on leadership, is the founding chairman at the Leadership Institute at the University of Southern California, and the chairman of the Center for Public Leadership at the Harvard's Kennedy School of Government. In his most recent book, *Leading for a Lifetime*, cowritten by Robert Thomas, he examines dozens of leaders in diverse environments. In their analysis they list four key skills or competencies that they identify as pillars of leadership. Those are: Adaptive Capacity, Engaging Others in a Shared Meaning, Distinctive Voice, and Integrity. They assert that the final prong, **integrity**, is a common attribute found among the world's most influential leaders and is a critical characteristic in those who wish to lead effectively through their lifetime.

In their book, Bennis and Thomas break the concept of integrity into three distinct legs that are strikingly similar to what Kouzes and Posner describe as elements of credibility: competence, a moral compass, and ambition. They caution that if, "any single element dominates [a] leader's behavior…he or she is at risk of lacking integrity"[17] or, as I assert, credibility. The balance of these three elements is necessary for the credibility, success, and decency of every leader.

Leading for a Lifetime defined competence, or **expertise**, as including the acquisition and mastery of specific skills. The **moral compass** leg of the tripod, which includes honesty and trustworthiness, must be of equal length for the tripod to stand. Bennis and Thomas cite to Shakespeare's character, Hamlet, to illustrate this point. They write, "[h]e was highly principled but feckless, thrusting his sword in all the wrong places and killing off the innocents as well as the indifferent..."[18] One must only recount the reigns of Hitler, Stalin, Lenin, or Mao to realize that a leader with high ambition and exceptional competence in their field can become "venomous pied pipers," who lead their followers to participate in atrocious and unthinkable behavior.[19] A leader will be more influential and have a *positive* and lasting impact if they can effectively balance their ambition and competence with a moral compass.[20]

Lastly, and where they diverge from Kouzes and Posner, Bennis and Thomas hold that **ambition** is also a needed source of integrity. Ambition is, "the desire to achieve something, whether for personal gain or the good of the community or both."[21] Self-imposed and reasonable boundaries to a leader's aspirations are crucial to the stability of the integrity tripod. When ambition is unbridled, a leader runs the risk of making unethical choices and taking reckless or dangerous steps. There are countless examples that demonstrate how unchecked ambition can easily become a detrimental force, ranging from Albert J. Dunlap, an executive who forged his credentials in order to fraudulently gain a position as CEO for Sunbeam Corporation, to the collapse of Enron because of egregious misrepresentation of company financial conditions that led to bankruptcy. As Bennis and Thomas succinctly put it, "[a]mbition, absent a moral compass, is naked destructiveness,"[22] and certainly does not generate credibility.

c. Source Credibility

The final area of research we will examine is that of "source credibility." The credibility of a source of information determines how a message will be received. Our society, clients, and certainly our professional peers are generally skeptical. Lawyers question the source of statistics, ideas, and arguments. We are quick to be cynical and are difficult to convince. However, virtually everyone adheres to one simple concept that empirical research has validated: a person with more knowledge and experience, a person who is perceived as more trustworthy and honest, and someone who is dynamic and enthusiastic about an issue is more credible.

The earliest research on source credibility investigated how modifications in source characteristics influenced people's willingness to alter their attitudes on certain topics.[23] Carl Hovland and his associates ran a series of experiments, while working for Yale University and the U.S. Army during World War II, to determine what combinations of communicative abilities induced a change of attitude in subjects. In these early investigations, the source was typically defined as an individual mass communicator, such as a newscaster or world leader. The research measured a subject's attitude on an issue; exposed the subject to manipulated messages based on different source qualities; and then measured changes of attitude after the exposure. An individual or institution deemed credible had greater power to change attitudes than a source determined to be less credible. Source **expertise** and **trustworthiness** were determined to be the two central attributes of credibility. Additional source credibility studies have identified other notable characteristics of credibility, but a third critical, and commonly cited, characteristic is the **dynamism** of the speaker. Several studies have shown that a speaker's dynamic approach or attraction to the audience, which involves more than physical appearance, lends significant credibility to the message.[24]

Even if these factors are described in slightly different terms in the academic literature, there is a clear consensus in this area of research: the perceived credibility of a source makes a significant and deep-seeded difference in the acceptance of new attitudes and new behaviors among an audience. Presidents, politicians, CEOs, lawyers, and leaders have the ability to persuade when they are dynamic, and can connect with their audience, their ability to persuade increases dramatically.

The 2008 Democratic Primary shows the interplay of these three credibility traits. Senator Barack Obama is a vibrant and inspirational speaker who connects emotionally with much of his audience. One may not agree with his policies, but many people react positively to his message because of his dynamism. Yet, as Senator Hillary Clinton correctly pointed out, Senator Obama did not have the same level of experience and expertise as she did. Therefore, Senator Obama's credibility was weakest in terms of expertise. Similarly, while Hillary Clinton had more experience, she was not received as inspirational, and in some instances had problems with a negative perception for honesty.

Credibility plays out in the highest level of politics as well as in our daily practice. Credibility is important in our everyday experiences trying to persuade a peer, a client, a board of directors, or opposing counsel on an issue. A leader will deliberately build their source credibility by improving, and being conscious of, their reputation for honesty, expertise, and dynamism.

2. Credibility: What Does It Mean for Our Profession?

After a review of the most well-established research on what makes a person credible, three basic recurring themes emerge; a lawyer with credibility operates with **integrity**, is an **expert** in their field, and is **dynamic and inspiring**. While some would include Vision and Ambition as elements necessary of credibility, we will focus on the three most common characteristics deemed to establish and reinforce a person's credibility with their audience. Ambition and

Vision are important to a Leading Lawyer, beyond credibility, and are deserving of their own discussion in later chapters. Ambition is discussed as a part of drive and determination and vision is a key segment of creative thinking and a vision for positive change. Credibility, which is established by honesty, expertise, and a dynamic and inspirational commitment to the project at hand, is a necessary element to the success of the Leading Lawyer.

Here is an overview of how the elements of credibility apply to the legal profession:[25]

CHARACTERISTICS THAT DESCRIBE A CREDIBLE LEADING LAWYER

Competence	Trustworthiness	Dynamism/Inspiration
Has in-depth knowledge of the law and the subject matter and has a broad base of information.	Gives honest and effective information and feedback.	Has high energy. Relates positively to clients, parties, attorneys, judges, and constituents.
Can reference significant and relevant subject matter publications and precedents; has industry knowledge and far-reaching understanding of the law and the industry.	Follows through on promises. Does what he says he will do.	Enthusiastic about the issues, the problems, and solutions. (note: this is not charisma—it is a display of serious and dynamic interest in the issues at hand)
Proven track record of success in the subject area.	Objective and looks at issues from multiple perspectives.	Has good presentation skills and is secure and appropriate in all aspects of communications.
Communicates well and has the ability to answer sophisticated questions and can explain complex issues well.	Sincere and willing to acknowledge problems. Flexible, adaptive, and committed.	Interesting and flexible in the communication process.
Trained, Professional, Experienced	Honest, Sincere, Realistic	Appealing, Respectful, Expressive

We sometimes underestimate the value of honesty, expertise, and inspiration to our careers and sometimes naively believe that we already have all of these traits. Even if you do embody all of the elements that make a lawyer

credible in the eyes of your constituents, the Leading Lawyers that I have interviewed treat these characteristics as areas for continuous improvement.

a. Honesty, Integrity, and Trustworthiness

The first prong of credibility is known by many names such as integrity,
honesty, trustworthiness, and candor. Whatever label you choose, you cannot underestimate the significance of integrity to the success of any situation.
Specifically, trustworthiness is one of the most important tenets of the legal
profession. We must constantly remind ourselves of the importance of integrity at an individual and institutional level. In this sense, we can improve our
individual and organizational characters by creating an environment that encourages honesty and promotes high standards. Integrity is at the core of every
successful legal institution.

Currently, there is a growing educational movement to teach values and
ideals in elementary and high schools.[26] Law schools teach the ABA's Model
Rules of Professional Conduct (MRPC) and there has been a trend toward extensive training in the workplace in areas such as sexual harassment, diversity,
affirmative action, sensitivity training, and employee standards of conduct.[27]
But, integrity is more than HR training sessions or passing the ethics section
of the bar exam; it requires the internalization of higher principles and the
consistent display of honesty and trustworthiness. The legal standard requires
that lawyers act ethically which, at a minimum, demands compliance with the
ABA's MRPC. However, character and integrity are more than ethics. Integrity
is doing the "right" thing *every time*, even when not bound to do so by baseline
ethical requirements.

Former congressman and White House chief of staff to President Bill Clinton, Leon Panetta, situates this overriding imperative to educate for integrity
as another part of his mission to lead. The process of instilling and assessing
values is critical to a law school education and is never finished:

> *I remember when I was in law school. …The people who*
> *succeeded were the people who always had that higher view*
> *of their role as lawyers, and I never forgot that. …[Many]*
> *factors determine what your value set is going to be like; but*
> *if you can find a way in law school to say, "These are the sets*
> *of values that you ought to have, as an attorney, and this is*
> *right, and this is wrong, and this is how a problem should*
> *play out." If you find a way to do that then law school and*
> *the practice of law can be a hell of a lot more meaningful.* [28]

The personal character of lawyers and leaders is at the core of all professional leadership effectiveness.[29] We are all aware of how persuasive a credible source can be. A reputation for honesty and trustworthiness establishes credibility with clients as well as opposing counsel, their clients, and judges that cannot be accomplished by expertise or dynamism alone. In showing your client that you can be trusted to assess a situation with candor and advise them of their options with an eye toward their best interests, you encourage loyalty and engender the type of relationship needed to create positive change.

As defined by former General Counsel for GE Ben Heineman for a corporation, integrity is:

> *a tenacious adherence on the part of the corporation to the spirit and the letter of the formal rules, financial and legal, voluntary adoption of global ethical standards that bind the company and its employees to act in its enlightened self-interest, and employee commitment to the core values of honesty, candor, fairness, reliability, and trustworthiness – values which infuse the creation and delivery of products and services and which guide internal and external relationships.*[30]

While this definition was constructed in order to describe integrity in a multinational corporation with several business lines, it is easy to see how it can be applied directly to the legal profession at both an individual and organizational level. Therefore, integrity in the legal arena, is 1) a tenacious adherence on the part of legal counsel to the spirit and letter of the law; 2) a voluntary adoption of the highest ethical and moral standards that bind counsel and their constituents to act for their clients enlightened self-interest; and 3) a commitment to the core values of honesty, fairness, and trustworthiness in their endeavors.

The benefits of integrity are numerous and far-reaching.[31] Inside an organization, it helps attract and retain top talent, empower employees to speak up on both performance and integrity concerns, and contribute to talent and merit-based employment practices. Operating with integrity helps create a culture of alignment between personal values and company values, thus improving morale, pride in the company, and productivity. In the marketplace, it enhances the firm's "brand," contributes to the trustworthiness of the firm's services, differentiates the organization from its competitors, and advances growth. In broader society, it enhances the firm's reputation and provides a positive example of lawyers as leaders in the community.

b. How to Build Personal Integrity

The easiest way to continue with good character development is to behave honestly and perform in manners consistent with your word.[32] Robert Grey says it this way: "[I]t starts when your word is your bond. When you tell someone you are going to do something you follow through. And if you're unable to follow through, you communicate that to them."[33] People who have honest attitudes to which their behavior conforms[34] are ahead of the game. Many people have learned this through life experiences but participation in a training process that provides a positive way of thinking and teaches desirable behaviors and skills is always useful.[35] Leading Lawyers proactively seek exceptional behavioral methods and are open to improvement.

It is also helpful to take on a role as a leader. After accepting the task of leader, build a climate of trust and honesty. Take the time to improve and find out how other people perceive your character and work to gain their trust. Feedback can come from many places, a mentor, a trusted colleague, or adopt a feedback process to get honest input. [36] Improve your interpersonal skills by attending skill building programs. To act with integrity, you must first develop your own standards. "You must know what you stand for, what you believe in, and what you care most about. Clarity of values will give you the confidence to make the tough decisions, to act with determination, and to take charge of your life."[37] When you learn and adopt positive behaviors, there is an improvement of attitude and character. Those that have high character and integrity and act consistently with their word model the core values of the profession.[38]

Furthermore, you can look to other leaders with noteworthy attributes and adopt the traits that you admire most. Compare and analyze the attributes of people whom you consider to be "great" leaders and those you feel are "poor" leaders. Seek out challenging and different and diverse assignments to build your character and knowledge base. Read biographies of great leaders and look for lessons in hardship and adversity. Finally, self-evaluate your performance and habits and compare your assessment with the organization's assessment.

Those with high levels of character and integrity:[38]	Those with low levels of character and integrity:
Act consistently with their word	Fail to follow through
Avoid saying one thing and doing another	Are threatened by others' success
Follow through on promises and commitments	Make themselves look good at the expense of others
Model the core values of the profession	Constantly walk the line of ethical behavior and sometimes walk below it
Lead by example	Make exceptions for themselves

c. How to Generate Integrity Within an Organization

Establishing a culture of integrity is essential to the success of any organization, especially a legal organization. Generally speaking, there are two common cultures: One is a punishment-oriented culture, where people are afraid of violating company rules, getting caught, and being punished. The other culture is an integrity-culture, where affirmative values and norms of behavior are so widely shared that people want to succeed the right way. It is easy to guess that a culture of integrity, as opposed to one that is punishment-oriented, is likely to yield better results. An integrity culture is created as much by aspirations, examples, transparency, and incentives as it is by penalties.[39] Giving the time and effort needed to embed integrity into the culture is challenging for busy law firms[40] and lawyers, but it is necessary to build credibility.

Heineman in his book, *High Performance with High Integrity*, and Gene Klann in his book, *Building Character*, recommend several ways in which an organization can work to build character and integrity within an organization.

i. Demonstrate Commitment

Leading Lawyers embody the level of integrity they seek from their colleagues and the organizations highest-profile leaders must display this commitment. The organization's leaders must exemplify the values expected from others or hypocrisy will undermine their credibility. Consistency in a leaders' actions is important because leaders are judged by how they spend their time, how they react in high-pressure or critical situations, the stories they tell, the questions they ask, the language they choose, and the measures they use. In "walking the walk," leaders can then demand personal behavior of others that is consistent with their espoused values.

ii. Communicate Integrity at All Levels

Those who seek to create an organization of integrity must then communicate and implement related practices at all levels. Furthermore, they must be willing to enforce those standards at the highest levels. Do not spare, excuse, or favor higher-level team members, but hold them every bit as accountable for lapses in integrity as they would be for other performance standards. This standard was upheld at GE in the early '90s when a scandal arose with their Foreign Military Sales Program. Not only were lower-level employees removed but so was the highly respected head of the division in charge of that program. This sent the message that there were consequences at all levels for a breach of integrity.[41]

iii. Make Integrity Part of the Process

Make operating with integrity an automatic part of all decision-making processes. This includes legal decisions and advice on behalf of clients as well as business decisions which affect the direction of the organization. Confront the complexity in the law, and in practice, with the understanding that the law needs to be followed in the spirit with which it was written.[42] Develop a system or process to prevent, detect, and respond to situations that implicate issues of integrity. Have clear, written, and feasible organizational values. [43]

iv. Adopt the Highest Ethical Standards

Adopt the highest moral and ethical standards practiced. Understand that the ABA's MRPC is the baseline for ethical behavior required of lawyers. Go beyond this minimum standard and seek to create positive change for your client and other stakeholders.

Challenge tactics that, although technically legal, are questionable to one's values. One of the difficult issues that Ben Heineman had to deal with at GE was whether or not they could continue to do business in Iran and Burma. He took a conservative and ethical approach to the Foreign Corrupt Practices Act and determined GE could not, even though this hurt many of their business partners and the company's bottom line. [44] Robert Grey once said that "[t]here has always been and...there will always be a movement in our profession to keep the bar of professionalism as high as possible. If we become [just] another business, then that professionalism tends to disappear and the minimum standard of ethics then becomes the norm."[45]

v. Stay Ahead of Ethical Trends and Expectations

Monitor fast-moving financial and legal rules. Leading Lawyers should continually mine sources for developments in ethical standards that affect their case or deal. These include new and pending legislation and regulation, filed and newly decided lawsuits, formal and informal government investigations, industry debates, criticisms, and media reports on all of the above.[46] Because integrity extends beyond formal financial and legal requirements, demands for higher standards are emerging at an increasing rate from a wide range of stakeholders. In monitoring the current trends, you can avoid even the appearance of impropriety.

vi. Be a Partner and a Guardian

As counsel, it is your job to help your client and organization understand how the law can be used affirmatively and strategically in a wide variety of ways. In playing the Partner Role, this includes achieving business goals as quickly and effectively as possible, doing informative and constructive due diligence, helping to negotiate transactions, simplifying contracts while retaining needed protections, and helping to influence significant policy debates.[47] In the Guardian Role, an in-house lawyer must resist giving the kinds of quick, simplistic answers that may seem necessary in fast-moving, complex situations.[48] Advice must be given in order to comply with law and regulations across the world, shape the companies governance rules, and ultimately deal with the public interests affected by the corporation's actions. Of course, when presented with a black-and-white issue of integrity, you can and should answer quickly and forcefully. Use your experience and wisdom to give the go-ahead when you strongly support a proposed moved and be as equally strong when you oppose it.[49]

As Heineman puts it, "counsel must be unafraid to answer candidly or argue back, undaunted by personal or group pressure, and be secure within their thick skins. They cannot let their views be summarily dismissed in the heat of battle. They have to get those views on the table, understood, and considered in the decision process."[50] Importantly, Heineman also suggests that the dual role of the Partner and Guardian, in the right circumstance and with client involvement, also applies to private firm lawyers. An outside lawyer should not be a yes-man on business issues or just a naysayer on legal issues.[51]

vii. Foster Awareness, Knowledge, and Commitment

The organization and team leaders need to help their employees and members become aware of integrity risks and consequences, show them how to find the right answer, and reinforce their commitment to do the right thing.[52] The first and most critical step to educating and training constituents about integrity is articulating what they *should do*.[53] Underscore that these issues are real by instituting a tracking, training, or testing system, all of which are essential to force people to grapple with competing considerations, to try on different roles, and to look for alternative ways to approach problems.[54] Identify strengths and weaknesses in order to maintain the strengths and improve upon the weaknesses. Use performance appraisals and give balanced feedback in order to avoid negativity but maintain a system of discipline.[55]

Organizations can design programs that do not heap scorn on legacy culture but rather explain why those practices are unacceptable in today's society and economy.[56] Furthermore, veteran lawyers should challenge junior lawyers with job assignments that will grow and develop their leadership skills and build character. Not every assignment will require a major decision but developmental assignments gradually improve skills by encouraging a strong ethics and the management of stress. Provide hands-on training, accommodate different learning styles with lectures or visual representations, and suggest books or biographies that team members can read for continued self-education.[57] Encourage learning from adversity and hardship rather than allowing such setbacks to have a negative impact on the person.[58]

viii. Give Employees a Voice

Encourage and require the reporting of concerns about possible violations of financial, legal, and ethical standards, and address those concerns promptly.[59] Discipline or terminate those who fail to act honestly or below ethical standards and do not retaliate against those who do.[60] Perform periodic integrity reviews and treat all integrity concerns with respect and professionalism.[61] In doing so, you send a potent message about the importance of a self-cleansing culture: one that promptly surfaces what is wrong and candidly discusses what is right.[62]

ix. Pay for Performance with Integrity

Discuss specific annual integrity objectives with employees and identify them as a basis for compensation. Systematically evaluate them at year end, just as with performance goals.[63] Conduct audits, take surveys, participate in and initiate integrity reviews, and generate self-assessment tools to use in the interim. Compare your organization with peer organizations, or former assessments of industry standards and best practices. Furthermore, personalized goals and objectives plus explicit integrity guidelines—which affect a component of pay and are factors in promotions—provide essential, real-world incentives that can have a significant role in creating the high-performance-with-high-integrity culture.[64]

Operating with integrity is only one component of an individual or organization's integrity. Being an expert in the relevant fields will also substantially boost your credibility as a Leading Lawyer and there are effective ways in which to showcase and build that expertise.

d. Competence and Expertise

Credibility requires both technical competence *and* leadership competence. Technical competence is the knowledge, experience, and ability to perform the task at hand or to provide the appropriate in-depth analysis. This technical ability and the drive to become an expert is one of the most important elements of credibility and it provides a measurable gauge for improvement. Build your credibility by becoming an expert in your field. Become an expert on the cases, statutes, industry publications, treatises, and gather as much information as you can about the business of your clients. Display this knowledge by writing articles, being published in industry publications, and participating in industry panels or committees.

Your success depends on your persuasion, and in most settings, your persuasiveness will increase when you can demonstrate the technical competence and experience needed to implement a business or legal solution or to litigate a difficult case. Fortunately, this is one of the simplest things to work on. Leading Lawyers have the Drive and Determination necessary to become an expert in their field as, explained further in Chapter Four, and they continue to work on their knowledge and skills.

The second component, leadership competence, will also boost your credibility with your clients, organization, and constituents. "Expertise in leadership skills per se is another dimension of competence. The abilities to challenge, inspire, enable, act as a model, and encourage...must be demonstrated if leaders are to be seen as capable."[65] For someone to enlist with you in a joint effort, your overall leadership competence, in addition to technical expertise, is crucial to exhibit previous successes. It is helpful to demonstrate your winning track record, successes on similar projects, and your ability to lead your client or organization in the proposed endeavor. It is significant that you take the time to learn the business, the law, and to know your client's current operation as best as you can.[66] Leading Lawyers will seek to be the best in their field, continually seek new insights into leadership, and will further educate themselves in all the important skills and knowledge areas.

e. Dynamic and Inspiring

The third, and last, component of credibility for Leading Lawyers is the ability to be dynamic and inspiring. Dynamism is described as a "great energy or enthusiasm"[67] for whatever topic or issue is being discussed. In a written report for the University of Oklahoma Program for Instructional Innovation by Arletta Knight, Ph.D., she states that, "[d]ynamism focuses on the [speaker's] "passion"...It also involves the presentation skills of the speaker. ... a dynamic [speaker] is one who is more likely to be confident, articulate, and animated."[68] However, she goes on to say that "credibility is determined, not just by...behavior, but by the [audience's] interpretation of the meaning of that behavior."[69] Dynamism is more than mere charisma; it is a speaker's ability to convey his enthusiasm and commitment to the task at hand. A Leading Lawyer is dynamic and by this we do not just mean charismatic.

A leader is also inspiring. We admire and respect leaders who are uplifting, enthusiastic, positive, and optimistic. A credible leader has the ability to "bolster people's self-efficacy and foster greater self-confidence."[70] A Leading Lawyer not only has faith in their solutions and vision but can communicate that belief in a way that allows constituents to believe in them as well. Effective leaders will also communicate confidence in the success of their constituents. Having confidence and believing in our own ability to handle the job, and trusting the ability of our constituents, no matter how difficult, is essential to promoting and sustaining consistent efforts.[71] It is a leader's challenge to create situations for small wins, structuring tasks in such a way that they can be broken down into manageable pieces, with each success building up the person's sense of competence.[72]

When leaders act in ways that uplift our spirits and restore our belief in the future, they strengthen their own personal credibility.[73] Constituents look for leaders who demonstrate an enthusiastic and genuine belief in the capacity of others, who strengthen people's will, who supply the means to achieve, and who express optimism for the future.[74] Credible leaders sustain hope by painting positive images and solutions for the future. They arouse optimistic feelings and enable their constituents to hold positive thoughts about the possibilities of success.[75] Optimism is essential to strengthening credibility. In expressing their conviction that it will work out for the best and believing that the future will be better than the past, optimists instill confidence in others and they begin to adopt a similar attitude.[76]

3. Conclusion

It is important to understand that these elements and attributes of credibility can be learned and can always be improved upon. I remind my students regularly that credibility is the largest single factor of their success in the future. I advise them to become experts in an area of law in which they are interested; caution them to always act with the highest degree of integrity; and impress upon them the importance of mastering the craft of dynamic and inspirational communication of their ideas and views. These are skills available to students as well as the most experienced of practicing attorneys. When asked what he looks for when making hiring decisions at GE, Ben Heineman replied, "I sought, first, to recruit world class experts...But, I was also looking for people who had leadership skills and organizational skills...[lawyers with] concern about ethics and reputation, technical lawyering skill and an ability to communicate."[77] The strategic and balanced combination of integrity, expertise, and dynamism solidifies the Leading Lawyer's credibility with their clients, organization, opposing counsel and parties, and judges. Credibility is what we all look for in a Leading Lawyer.

Notes

1. James S. Kouzes and Barry Z. Posner, *The Leadership Challenge*, 27 Jossey-Bass (4th ed. 2007).

2. Oxford English Dictionary Online, http://www.oed.com/ (accessed May 5, 2008).

3. Ben W. Heineman, Jr., "Caught in the Middle", *Corporate Counsel*, 73 (April 2007).

4. James S. Kouzes and Barry Z. Posner, *The Leadership Challenge*, Jossey-Bass (4th ed. 2007).

5. Warren Bennis and Robert Thomas, *Leading for a Lifetime*, Harvard Business School (2007).

6. James S. Kouzes and Barry Z. Posner, *The Leadership Challenge*, Jossey-Bass (4th ed. 2007).

7. James S. Kouzes and Barry Z. Posner, *The Leadership Challenge*, 27 Jossey-Bass (3rd ed. 2002).

8. *Id*. at 32.

9. Kouzes and Posner, *supra* note 4 at 29.

10. *Id*. at 40.

11. Kouzes and Posner, *supra* note 7 at 28.

12. *Id*. at 31.

13. *Id*. at 32.

14. *Id*. at 34.

15. *Id*. at 36.

16. Bennis and Thomas, *supra* note 5.

17. *Id*. at 146.

18. *Id*. at 148.

19. *Id*. at 149.

20. *Id*. at 150.

21. *Id*. at 145.

22. Bennis and Thomas, *supra* note 5 at 146.

23. *See, e.g.*, Carl I. Hovland, Irving L. Janis and Harold H. Kelley *Communication and Persuasion: Psychological Studies of Opinion Change*, Yale University Press (1953); Carl I. Hovland and Walter Weiss, "The Influence of Source Credibility on Communication Effectiveness", *Public Opinion Quarterly*, 15(1), 635-650 (1951).

24. David K Berlo, James B. Lemert and Robert J. Mertz, "Dimensions for Evaluating the Acceptability of Message Sources", *Public Opinion Quaterly* 46, 563-576 (March 1969) (noting a similar attribute, the attractiveness of the speaker, reflects dynamic, expressive, appealing, attractive, and exciting content); M. Eisend, "Source Credibility Dimensions in Marketing Communication – A Generalized Solution", *Journal of Empirical Generalizations in Marketing*, 22 (2006).

25. Chart adapted from: M. Eisend, Source "Credibility Dimensions in Marketing Communication – A Generalized Solution", *Journal of Empirical Generalizations in Marketing*, 22 (2006).

26. Character Education Partnership, http://www.character.org/ (accessed August 2008).

27. Gene Klann, *Building Character*, 3 Jossey-Bass (2007).

28. Interview with Leon Panetta, October 2006.

29. John H. Zenger and Joseph Folkman, The Extraordinary Leader: Turning Good Managers into Great Leaders, 12-13 McGraw-Hills (2002).

30. Ben W. Heineman, *High Performance with High Integrity*, 3 Harvard Business Press (2008).

31. *Id.* at 23-24.

32. Zenger and Folkman, *supra* note 29 at 79.

33. Interview with Robert Grey, July 2008.

34. Zenger and Folkman, *supra* note 32.

35. *Id.* at 80.

36. *Id.* at 233-234.

37. Kouzes and Posner, *supra* note 7.

38. Zenger and Folkman, *supra* note 29 at 103.

39. Heineman, *supra* note 30 at 25.

40. *Id.* at 37.

41. Interview with Ben W. Heineman, Jr., July 2008.

42. Heineman, *supra* note 30 at 44.

43. Klann, *supra* note 27 at 19.

44. Heineman, *supra* note 41.

45. Interview with Robert Grey, July 2008.

46. Heineman, *supra* note 30 at 59.

47. *Id.* at 69.

48. *Id.* at 70.

49. *Id.*

50. *Id.* at 74.

51. Interview with Ben W. Heineman, Jr., August 2008.

52. Heineman, *supra* note 30 at 76.

53. *Id.* at 78.

54. *Id.* at 82.

55. Klann, *supra* note 27 at 19.

56. Heineman, *supra* note 30 at 84.

57. Klann, *supra* note 27 at 19.

58. *Id.*

59. Heineman, *supra* note 30 at 86.

60. *Id.* at 88-89.

61. *Id.* at 93.

62. *Id.*

63. *Id.* at 95.

64. *Id.* at 99.

65. James S. Kouzes and Barry Z. Posner, *Credibility: How Leaders Gain and Lose It, Why People Demand It*, 18 Jossey-Bass (2003).

66. *Id.* at 17.

67. Dictionary.com, http://dictionary.reference.com/browse/dynamism (accessed September 2008).

68. Arletta Knight, University of Oklahoma Program for Instructional Innovation, "Teacher 'Credibility': A Tool for Diagnosing Problems in Teacher/Student Relationships" *available at* www.ou.edu/pii/tips/ideas/credibility.html.

69. *Id.*

70. Kouzes and Posner, *supra* note 65 at 164.

71. *Id.* at 167-168.

72. *Id.* at 167.

73. *Id.* at 218.

74. *Id.*

75. Kouzes and Posner, *supra* note 65 at 221.

76. *Id.* at 203.

77. Interview with Ben Heineman, July 2008.

CHAPTER FOUR:
Use Drive and Determination

The first step to becoming a Leading Lawyer is building the credibility that is indispensable to effectively championing the client's needs and creating positive change through the influence and persuasion of others. The next important step is that you have to *want* to become successful as a lawyer and a leader. The lawyers who flourish have a willingness and dedication to hard work, to become experts, and to serve as instruments of positive change. They lead by example, accept responsibility (in fact they want responsibility), and adapt to changing circumstances. After passion inspires them, they have the persistence to facilitate change. In everyday situations, as well as in crisis, Leading Lawyers have drive and determination.

Supreme Court Justice Joyce Kennard has always had amazing drive and determination; in life, in her pursuit of a quality education, and in her work. During her youth, she demonstrated a work ethic and adaptability that eventually led her to a position as a justice of the California Supreme Court; she has shown what it means to lead by example, accept responsibility, and become a brilliant instrument of change. Justice Kennard is the personification of drive and determination.

From an early age she recognized that an education would provide her with the opportunity she needed to be self-sufficient. Born during WWII, she spent her early childhood

"On that long road to success, and I emphasize the word long, you will stumble. You have the choice of remaining on the ground or you can pick yourself up, and struggle again on that path that you hope will take you to the career or the success that you have dreamed of. Don't give up, just persevere."

Justice Joyce Kennard
Associate Justice of the
California Supreme Court

"Leadership requires a certain amount of fire in the belly, to think big and creatively, as well as the courage to set a high goal and stick with it."

Fred Krupp
President of the
Environmental Defense Fund

in a concentration camp with her mother. Her father passed away in the camp when she was just one year old. It was not until years later, when she and her mother moved to the last remaining Dutch colony in New Guinea, that Justice Kennard would attend a tiny school run by Catholic missionaries. The school closed when she was just 13 prompting yet another move in the hopes of just one more year of schooling.

In my interview with Justice Kennard, she spoke of how woefully inadequate her early education had been. However, with the rudiments of an education, Kennard's mother moved her to Holland and was able to secure her admittance into a high school on the condition that she receive special tutoring in math to remain with her class. Only six months later, Kennard's education was again abruptly interrupted. She had developed a tumor that required amputation of her leg above the knee. Despite the diligence with which she approached her studies, her surgery and the necessary recovery closed the door on Kennard's high school education. However, instead of admitting defeat, Kennard acquired a job as a secretary at the young age of 16.

Always on the lookout for an opportunity to continue her education, Kennard moved one last time in search of her dream. She immigrated to America in 1961 when a quota was established for people of Dutch nationality from New Guinea who were displaced by the Indonesian independence. Kennard arrived in the country alone and took another job, this time as a legal secretary. Six years later, Justice Kennard's mother passed away, leaving her a small savings of $5,000. Kennard realized that this was possibly her last opportunity to realize her dream of earning a college degree. Seizing the opportunity in the midst of her grief, she reduced her hours to part-time and enrolled in a community college as a 27-year-old freshman. She went on to complete four years worth of undergraduate courses in only three years. Despite this grueling schedule, Justice Kennard persevered. She not only earned her degree from the University of Southern California in German, but graduated magna cum laude and Phi Beta Kappa.

After graduation, Kennard's boss encouraged her to continue her studies and become a lawyer herself. She decided to pursue a joint degree program in law and public administration from the University of Southern California. Using her degree, she gained legal experience in the State Attorney General's Office and later as a research attorney for the State Court of Appeal. By the mid-'80s, she was appointed to the bench of the Los Angeles Municipal Court. In three short years, Kennard was advanced to the State's superior court, the

Court of Appeal, and finally in 1989, appointed by the governor to the Supreme Court.

Today, she is the longest-sitting justice on the California Supreme Court, having been retained by voters in 1994 and again in 2006. Despite her long years of service to the court she remains intimately committed to her work. Justice Kennard corrects each one of her opinions as many as 15 times before signing her name to ensure that it is as clear, accurate, and concise as it can possibly be. By her example of working closely with her research attorneys and clerks, she is a brilliant reflection of how drive and determination can make a lawyer a leader.

Not everyone can have such an amazing story as Justice Kennard. How do the components of drive and determination apply in a more typical career?

1. Leading Lawyers Have the Drive to Become Experts, Lead by Example, and Advocate High Standards

Leading Lawyers strive for continuous improvement in themselves, others, and the organization for which they work. They lead by example and follow through with their commitments. A Leading Lawyer expects and demands high levels of performance and works to become an expert in their field.

Larry Sonsini would agree that gaining and maintaining expertise in one's field is of vital importance to a lawyer's success. Leading Lawyers continually seek a deeper and more comprehensive understanding of the nuisances of their practice and their curiosity and drive to be the best propels them to search for new learning opportunities. Sonsini's drive and determination to remain a leader in his field is exemplified through his dedication to keep up with his education by becoming an educator himself. In speaking about his love for teaching law at Boalt Hall for 20 years, Sonsini said:

> And one of the reasons why I love[d] teaching, …(was) the fact that I was reading cases again, and I felt that was important, and I had an obligation which I imposed on myself. Even to this day, if there is a statute that is relevant, I don't feel good about it myself unless I read it.[1]

Larry Sonsini, like all Leading Lawyers, has a thirst for knowledge that cannot be quenched.

As Leading Lawyers relentlessly pursue superiority in their legal fields, they also exhibit a determination to be a model of excellence. Peter Drucker was one of the most influential business minds of the past century, consulting for large companies such as General Motors, General Electric, Intel, Coca-Cola, Citicorp, and IBM. During his years as a consultant he found that there were many different types of successful leaders with varying leadership styles. He discovered that some leaders were aloof while others were more down to earth; some were gregarious while others would seclude themselves in their executive offices. However, Drucker noted that all of the successful leaders had submitted themselves to the "mirror test" – that is, they made sure that the person they saw in the mirror in the morning was the kind of person they wanted to be. This is the way they fortified themselves against the leader's greatest temptations: to do things that are popular rather than do things that are right.[2] Similarly, in *The Leadership Challenge*, James Kouzes and Barry Posner advise that prior to leading by example you must first fully comprehend your own values, beliefs, and assumptions that drive you forward. Once you have freely identified and chosen the principles that will guide your actions, you can more clearly communicate your goals. Before you can do what you say, you must be sure that you mean what you say.[3] Once a Leading Lawyer has solidified their guiding principles they can demonstrate their intense commitment to their beliefs with each and every action. A Leading Lawyer must themselves be willing to make the same changes and sacrifices that they demand of their constituents.[4]

Moreover, a leader who hopes to be successful must be present in the process, pay close attention to progress and setbacks, and participate directly in the selected course of action in order to accomplish extraordinary things. Leaders take every opportunity to show others by their own example that they are deeply committed to the values and aspirations they espouse.[5] How you spend your time is the single clearest indicator, especially to other people, about what is important to you.[6] For instance, in an interview with Fred Krupp, president of the Environmental Defense Fund, he spoke about an attorney in their Colorado office named Vickie Patton. He said of Patton that she is:

> *...one of the handful of people in the whole nation...that understand the working of the Clean Air Act. She has made cleaning America's skies her goal. She's been involved in cases all the way to the Supreme Court of the United States...(and)*

thanks to her work, and that of other lawyers that she's worked with, (she was) able to get the Bush Administration to propose something called the Clean Air Interstate Rule…(which) will reduce sulfur and nitrogen pollution in (America), at least in the eastern 29 states, by 70 percent.[7]

Patton is dedicated to her goal and demonstrates her dedication through her expertise, hard work, and persistence in creating positive change. A Leading Lawyer will consciously choose to devote time and energy on the aspects that they find most important and essential to their success.

A Leading Lawyer also sets high standards and lives by them. As John Gardner, founder of Common Cause, a member of President Johnson's cabinet, and Presidential Medal of Honor recipient, pointed out in his book *Excellence*, "[w]hen we raise our sights, strive for excellence, dedicate ourselves to the highest goals of our society, we are enrolling in an ancient and meaningful cause – the age-long struggle of humans to realize the best that is in them."[8] Leaders will seek out those who are most qualified to help them pursue positive change. Great leaders understand that reaching lofty goals often requires enlisting the skills and qualities constituents but they do not view their dependence on others as a weakness; "[t]hey (are) not afraid of the strengths in their associates. They glor[y] in it."[9] The motto that a Leading Lawyer lives by is that which Andrew Carnegie wished to have engraved on his tombstone: "Here lies a man who attracted better people into his service than he was himself."[10] Leading Lawyers feel an obligation to set the bar high and to make every effort to show their followers how to reach that bar; by trying to reach for it themselves.

2. Leading Lawyers Initiate and Accept Responsibility

Leading Lawyers do not just pay lip service to the idea of change, they take personal responsibility to make sure deadlines and goals are met and change is actually implemented. A leader makes a choice "to take a chance, to be selfless, to take responsibility, to start something new, to do the right thing."[11] As a historical example:

On March 5, 1770, a confrontation between British soldiers and a crowd of Bostonians led to the death of five colo-

> *nists – the so-called Boston Massacre. Fearing popular anger,*
> *three lawyers in succession refused to serve as defense coun-*
> *sel. [But] John Adams thought it of great importance that*
> *the guilt or innocence of the soldiers be determined by a fair*
> *trial. Despite the fact that he was an influential member of the*
> *people's party, [and] anything but sympathetic to the Crown,*
> *he believed it was his responsibility to accept the defense as-*
> *signment.*[12]

A Leading Lawyer has an impulse to exercise initiative in social situations, to bear the burden of making the decision, to step forward when no one else will.[13]

In Panetta's view, Leading Lawyers have a critical responsibility not just to be zealous advocates for their clients, but to the larger system of law in which they operate.

> *It's very much like saying, if a patient has got some seri-*
> *ous heart problems, a cardiologist can't just walk away from*
> *that, or just say, "Well, send him to someplace or somebody*
> *else," or just tell the person to take two aspirin and go to bed.*
> *That person has a responsibility. In many ways, a lawyer has*
> *the same kind of responsibility, which is to stand back, and*
> *say in every situation, "I have a larger obligation to a system*
> *of justice that is essential to our democracy." They need to be*
> *trained. They need to have that larger set of values about their*
> *responsibilities.*

Similarly, after more than 60 years of business analysis, discussion, and observation, Peter Drucker concluded that each leader knew that "[l]eadership is not rank, privileges, titles, or money – it's responsibility."[14] Based on Drucker's model for business leadership, a Leading Lawyer should ask of themselves: What needs to be done? What is best for my client and their organization? What can and should I do to make a difference? What are my client's missions and goals? What constitutes performance and positive results for this organization? Leading Lawyers are not preachers, they are doers. They have the requisite hunger to seek untested paths but they also have the discipline and initiative necessary to achieve a desired goal.[15]

Any student of the life of President Lincoln would know that he too was a man of action. When Lincoln took office, he recognized how unprepared the Union was to engage the South in a civil war. The army was understaffed, undermanned, poorly equipped, and poorly trained. The sparse army of only 16,000 men was led by a 75-year-old general who relied on outdated warfare strategies and was physically incapable of commanding from the field. True to his leadership abilities, Lincoln took charge of the situation.

> Because there was such a paucity of military leadership in 1861, Lincoln was forced to formulate the nation's war policy himself. This included everything from drawing up war plans in the War Department offices to directing tactical movements in the field. In the four years that he was in office, Lincoln completely reorganized and redirected the Armed Forces of the United States. In fact, he increased the size of the army so substantially that at the end of the war, General Grant was in command of more than half a million men. Moreover, many of Lincoln's changes in the American military command system were permanent. And his overall design was later used as something of a blueprint for future reorganization.[16]

Lincoln would initiate major changes in the organization and leadership of the army when he felt that progress was not, or no longer, being made. Like Lincoln, a Leading Lawyer will not sit idly by and wait for someone else to accomplish a necessary task or reach an important goal; a Leading Lawyer will take the initiative and accept responsibility for making a positive change.

3. Leading Lawyers Are Familiar with Old-Fashioned Hard Work

As with anything in life, you will achieve greatness only through an enormous amount of hard work.[17] Scientific experts are producing remarkably consistent findings across a wide array of fields and there is no evidence of high-level performance without experience or practice.[18] Tiger Woods is a textbook example of what the research clearly shows. Because his father introduced him to golf at an extremely early age—18 months—and encouraged him to practice extensively, Woods had racked up at least 15 years of practice by the time he became the youngest-ever winner of the U.S. Amateur Championship at the age 18.[19] Woods has never stopped trying to improve, devoting many hours a day to conditioning and practice, even remaking his swing twice because that is what it took to get even better.[20] It is his drive to attain perfection and his persistent hard work that have made Woods, and allows him to remain, the extraordinary athlete that he is today.

Karl Llewellyn is another fine example of what dedication and hard work can accomplish. He was a professor at Columbia Law School from 1925 until 1951 and was heavily involved in a new movement called Legal Realism.[21] This group of Realists was distinguished by their contempt for those members of the legal profession who stated the law as though it were a body of black letter rules. Realists recognized that legal decision-making was often influenced by difficult facts or even irrational factors. These 'rule-skeptics' "criticized the older generation of treatise writers for failing to grapple with the uncertainty and ambiguity of doctrine."[22] They were actively involved in the reform movements that led to New Deal legislation, a new generation of treatises that included Corbin on Contracts and the Restatement projects of the American Law Institute. Llewellyn worked diligently to harmonize the varying laws among the states by drafting uniform codes and publishing Realist perspectives on the law. Through the 1940s, Llewellyn, in one of his greatest accomplishments of his career, took the lead in drafting the Uniform Commercial Code, "forging a single commercial code out of a chaotic welter of customs, statutes and decisions." He and his wife Soia Mentschikoff, partners in the UCC project, are credited with persuading legislators, lawyers and the business community to accept the new code.

The development and implementation of the UCC is truly a lesson in leadership. Llewellyn, as early as the 1920s, had identified problems in the legal profession that he sought to tackle. Over the next 10 to 15 years he participated in a wide variety of professional endeavors—working on Wall Street, litigating, writing legislation, involvement in scholarly societies, writing publications, and editing—to develop the skills that he believed would enhance his abilities to change his profession for the better. Llewellyn saw statutes not as legal Band-Aids but as a much needed frameworks and fertile starting points for fresh legal development.[23]

Llewellyn and the Realists are a great example of a group that saw the need for reform within their profession and achieved that reform—their positive change—by working hard and developing the skills required to do the job. The career of Karl Llewellyn provides a great example of a Leading Lawyer who identified the positive change he wanted to make and worked tirelessly to develop the characteristics and expertise necessary to bring about that change. Llewellyn, Woods, Kennard, and other Leading Lawyers are no strangers to the self-imposed discipline of hard work that is necessary for an extraordinary career. For Leading Lawyers, hard work comes with the territory.

4. Leading Lawyers Are Ambitious with a Capacity to Adapt

Leading Lawyers have the persistence to gain competence in their field or in the circumstances in which they hope to lead. They are decisive in their actions but are not stubbornly attached to methods or approaches that do not produce results. Their ambition and capacity to adapt to changing circumstances are what set a Leading Lawyer apart from their competition.

In Warren Bennis and Robert Thomas' book, *Leading for a Lifetime*, they state that an essential quality in a leader is a "voracious appetite for learning new things, coupled with an openness to new experiences."[24] Leaders are courageous and are continually seeking new solutions to problems. If one avenue fails, they will search for another; they can let go in order to move forward.[25] A leader must be aware of the degree to which they actually have the capabilities to do what they say. If they lack the requisite competence, they will dedicate themselves to acquiring the necessary expertise. As former ABA President Robert Grey points out:

> *We must adapt. Leaders develop themselves through associations, through reading, and through finding those personalities, those individuals who represent the characteristics they believe are important or through the important activities that have become known to them.*[26]

The amazing ability to adapt to new situations and maintain their ambition is what makes a Leading Lawyer more likely to successfully complete a complex or amorphous project.

Harnessing your ambition is critically dependent on some introspection that results in identifying the "authentic" you, setting your own standards, and not letting others set them for you. It requires self-confidence to set your own course, but if you can achieve that goal, life becomes easier. You are not working less, but you are enjoying the work more because you are no longer hostage to other people's opinions about what constitutes success.[27] Furthermore, a high-profile career is not the only ticket to success. Elizabeth Cabraser, a litigator who manages complex mass torts and securities class actions, believes that the lawyers that she admires the most are not always found in the big firms with high-profile careers. Cabraser would agree that Leading Lawyers are also found in small towns working as public defenders or working as community lawyers.[28]

Ambition and determination—the will to accomplish a goal, especially in the face of difficulties—are some of the more valuable passions a leader can have.[29] A Leading Lawyer has the drive and ambition to gain the requisite expertise and mastery of the specific skills necessary to the accomplishment of their goals.[30] It often manifests itself in a "can-do" attitude. A successful leader looks for ways to do things rather than looking for excuses that something will not work.[31] Surrounding yourself with a team of "can-do" determined people, rather than naysayers, will enable you to reach stretch goals together.[31] A Leading Lawyer fosters an attitude of success; instead of just trying to get something done, they aim to get better at it.[32]

It is important to recognize that while most people are willing to make an effort to solve easy problems, far fewer are willing to devote the mental effort, energy, and time to solving the more complex ones.[33] A leader's ability to avoid distraction, when faced with a worrisome situation that requires extraordinary efforts to eradicate, requires continued focus and commitment to the project. It requires the business savvy to separate the core of an issue from the ancillary matters and then to continue plugging away at the core.[34] It is also important to know when ambition and determination turn into stubbornness. Ambition requires a delicate balance between passionate dedication and blind obstinacy. Use your judgment to determine if your goal or vision needs to be modified or if a new approach should be constructed. If you feel progress is too slow or nonexistent, consider making changes or simplifying things; a Leading Lawyer is willing to modify their goal or course of action if necessary.

5. Leading Lawyers Seek Positive Change

Leading Lawyers have a strong moral compass and recognize their membership in a larger human community. They have values which they unflinchingly defend. Leaders seek out and eventually become mentors in order to leave the organization a better place than which it was found. Fred Krupp puts it this way: "Leadership is helping to change the real world and so it means, first and foremost, understanding the real world, …. doing your homework, understanding the nature of the problem to be solved, … asking the tough questions, and [taking] the most effective approach."[36] A Leading Lawyer has the desire to achieve something for the good of the community.[37] Positive ambition promotes the interests of your colleagues, your firm, your clients, and ultimately yourself.[38] A leader with ambition will search to find ways to make a difference. More often than not, the person who strives to make a positive impact *on other people* and does not constantly seek shorter routes to the next promotion is the one who will enjoy a sense of satisfaction that eludes those who are merely self-promoters.[39]

Bennis and Thomas wrote that people respond to a leader not because of any espoused religion or philosophy, but because of their conviction, their powerful sense of justice, and their passionate desire to do the right thing.[40] Kouzes and Posner hold that people admire most those who believe strongly in something, and who are willing to stand up for their beliefs.[41] Under normal circumstances, people prefer to give their allegiance to leaders of integrity. People know in their bones, or even their genes, it is the right thing to do.[42]

A moral path includes the desire to have a positive impact on the world.[43] Leading Lawyers, as their first thought, ask what they can do for others and their community. "Each time a man stands up for an ideal, or acts to improve the lots of others, or strikes out against injustice, he sends a tiny ripple of hope, and…those ripples build a current which can sweep down the mightiest walls of oppression and resistance."[44] For example, Elizabeth Cabraser was involved in a pro bono effort with a number of other firms that sought relief on behalf of Holocaust survivors as part of a worldwide class action in the federal court in the Eastern District of New York. The suit was filed against several Swiss banks that were still holding money and assets that had been taken from Jews and other ethnic groups during the Nazi regime. Through their combined efforts, Cabraser was able to help survivors come forward, to record their stories, and feel a sense of dignity in the courtroom that they would not otherwise have experienced in their home countries. Although no settlement agreement would have ever been enough to compensate for the suffering of millions of people, her clients were extremely grateful for the opportunity to tell their stories.[45] Leading Lawyers like Cabraser seek to leave the client or their organization in a better position than when they found it and create a positive change for the future.

One way to generate opportunity to create positive change is to seek a mentor. A good mentor will not only serve as a coach who provides valuable knowledge and perspective of the company and yourself, the mentor can also be an invaluable advocate for you within the organization.[46] Through a mentor, you can gain insights into an organization that would not otherwise be readily available and can then determine what aspects of the organization are in need of alteration. Becoming a mentor is another important way you can be a constructive influence on the future direction of an organization. Leading Lawyers take mentoring beyond mere supervision. They take the time to involve a mentee in their work, offering life lessons, and steering them through the corporate or legal culture in a positive way. Leading Lawyers are genuinely interested in their mentees' professional and personal success.[47] The only way the United States will again see the likes of Washington, Lincoln, and Roosevelt is by recognizing the unique contribution of those who put more selfish concerns on hold in order to serve some larger public good.[48]

6. Leading Lawyers Motivate and Inspire

Beyond their expertise, initiative, hard work, and ambition, leaders are optimists and purveyors of hope. Leading Lawyers are encouraging and provide the confidence that motivates individuals and organization to higher levels of performance. Even though they recognize the possibility of failure, leaders have an optimists' expectation of triumph. They see an arc to a desirable future that they believe they can travel. Leading Lawyers are convinced that their goal is worthy of the struggle and that they will prevail.[49] Without motivation and morale, we are unlikely to achieve excellence as a society or to provide the environment in which individual excellence can occur.[50] We will take a further look at motivation in Chapter Six on communication and persuasion but here are a few thoughts as it relates to drive and determination.

Leaders do not invent motivation in their followers, they unlock it. They work with the resources they are given.[51] Motivation is the ability to generate and keep yourself and your team energetic and enthused about the job and its challenges. However, what is the best way to motivate yourself and others? Research indicates clearly that measurement and feedback are essential to increase efforts to improve performance. Scorekeeping systems are essential to knowing how we are progressing.[52] Making goals public has a way of increasing our determination because we want to avoid the shame of failure. It also helps to persuade other constituents, such as other departments or customers, to become allies in helping us achieve our goals.[53] Optimism that our goals are attainable further helps to motivate and inspire great efforts to succeed.

Obviously, optimism can be carried to the point of the goal's detriment. Success requires a balance between a leader's optimism and pragmatism. Winston Churchill was a master at building the British people's confidence in themselves and understood that optimism must be tempered with realism. He said, "I have nothing to offer but blood, toil, tears and sweat." He was saying, as all great leaders must, that it was not going to be easy. He was also saying, what all leaders sooner or later find themselves saying—that failure is simply a reason to strengthen resolve.[54] "It is essential to society's health…that people have confidence in their institutions. While they do not need to believe that their society is perfect, they do need to believe that it is likely to meet their basic needs and confirm their values, or that at least they are moving in that direction."[1] Leading Lawyers seek to create a sense of morale that motivates their constituents to commit to achieving a shared goal through a realistic and achievable approach.

7. Conclusion

Drive and determination are hallmarks of the Leading Lawyer. It was the steady and unassuming theme underlying each interview that I conducted during my research. The concepts of becoming an expert, leading by example and advocating high standards, are second nature to Leading Lawyers like Fred Krupp and Larry Sonsini. Robert Grey clearly understands the significance of adaptability, Karl Llewellyn knew what it meant to work hard, and Winston Churchill appreciated the importance of inspiration. Likewise, all Leading Lawyers strive to create positive change in the lives of their clients and for the institutions they serve.

We have seen that credibility and drive and determination are the first steps in becoming a Leading Lawyer. However, what is one 'driving' toward? Leading Lawyers use their credibility and drive to follow opportunities, provide solutions, and create a vision for positive and ethical change.

NOTES

[1.] Interview with Larry Sonsini, August 2006.

2. Peter Drucker, "Leaders Are Doers", *Executive Excellence* (April 1996).

3. James S. Kouzes and Barry Z. Posner, *The Leadership Challenge*, 47-48 Jossey-Bass (4th ed. 2007).

4. *Id.* at 75-76.

5. *Id.*

6. *Id.* at 79.

7. Interview with Fred Krupp, July 2008.

8. John Gardner, *Excellence*, 160 W.W. Norton & Company, Inc. (1984).

9. Drucker, *supra* note 2.

10. *Id.*

11. Warren Bennis and Robert Thomas, *Leading for a Lifetime*, 105 Harvard Business School Press (2007).

12. John Gardner, *On Leadership*, 50 Free Press (1990).

13. *Id.* at 49.

14. Drucker, *supra* note 2.

15. Bennis and Thomas, *supra* note 11 at 102.

16. Donal Phillips, *Lincoln on Leadership*, 114-115 Warner Books (1992).

17. Geoffrey Colvin, "What it Takes to be Great", *Fortune* (October 2006), *available at* http://money.cnn.com/magazines/fortune/fortune_archive/2006/10/30/8391794/index.htm.

18. *Id.*

19. *Id.*

20. *Id.*

21. Mary Ann Glendon, *A Nation Under Lawyers*, 177-198 Harvard University Press (1994).

22. *Id.*

23. *Id.*

24. Bennis and Thomas, *supra* note 11 at xi.

25. *Id.*

26. Interview with Robert Grey, July 2008.

27. Tom Schimitt and Arnold Perl, *Simple Solutions*, 55-56 John Wiley & Sons, Inc. (2007).

28. Interview with Elizabeth Cabraser, August 2008.

29. Schimitt and Perl, *supra* note 27 at 195.

30. Bennis and Thomas, *supra* note 11 at 145.

31. Schimitt and Perl, *supra* note 27 at 195.

32. *Id.* at 196.

[33.] Colvin, *supra* note 17.

[34.] Schimitt and Perl, *supra* note 27 at 198.

[35.] *Id.*

[36.] Interview with Fred Krupp, July 2008.

[37.] Bennis and Thomas, *supra* note 11 at 145.

[38.] Schimitt and Perl, *supra* note 27 at 49.

[39.] *Id.* at 54.

[40.] Bennis and Thomas, *supra* note 11 at 142.

[41.] Kouzes and Posner, *supra* note 3 at 51-56.

[42.] Bennis and Thomas, *supra* note 11 at 142.

[43.] *Id.* at 144.

[44.] Bennis and Thomas, *supra* note 11 at 169.

[45.] Interview with Elizabeth Cabraser, August 2008.

[46.] Schimitt and Perl, *supra* note 27 at 58.

[47.] *Id.*

[48.] Bennis and Thomas, *supra* note 11 at 168.

[49.] *Id.* at 101.

[50.] Gardner, *supra* note 8 at 144.

[51.] *Id.* at 145.

[52.] Kouzes and Posner, *supra* note 3 at 92.

[53.] Schimitt and Perl, *supra* note 27 at 199-200.

[54.] Gardner, *supra* note 8 at 151.

[55.] *Id.* at 147.

CHAPTER FIVE:
Define a Vision and Practice Creative Thinking

In *The Leadership Challenge*, currently in its fourth edition with over 1.5 million copies sold, James Kouzes and Barry Posner conclude that one of the four most admired traits of a leader is their ability to **look forward**. This characteristic is common to Leading Lawyers, but not because they were trained in visionary or creative thinking in law school. Stare decisis is the foundation on which our theory of law and legal studies are based. It requires lawyers to look to the past for set precedents in order to delineate the rules that apply to a current fact pattern. Through education and practice we are taught to be great analytical thinkers. We spot the issues, parse the applicable rules, analyze the facts in accordance with the laws, and state our conclusions. However lawyers, in general, sometimes tend to overlook a key component that would allow for extraordinary accomplishment in their work: finding an early solution to a problem. Successful Leading Lawyers use their skills to look both backward *and* look forward because they are not merely concerned with precedent but with solutions for the future. Despite a lack of formal curriculum on creative and forward thinking, Leading Lawyers understand that a vision of the future, and a creative approach

"Looking forward? There is no other place to look. If you have to look back, if you have to look down, the whole purpose of doing both of those things is in order to look forward."

Mayor Rudy Giuliani
Former Mayor
of New York

"Leaders, in providing a vision, are able to help people internalize the challenge and to use their collective resources and talent to make what seems to be impossible, possible."

Robert Grey
Former President
of the American Bar
Association

63

to problem-solving, is what allows them to create and take advantage of opportunity for positive change.

Leading Lawyers use creative problem solving, forward thinking, and vision to help their clients solve problems and improve their organizations. They understand that their clients want short-term solutions to their immediate problems, long-term solutions to prevent future problems, advice for overall institutional improvement, in addition to traditional legal analysis. Clients expect their attorneys to analyze the legal situation appropriately, but Leading Lawyers go much further. Leading Lawyers analyze the law and participate in a process of finding a broader, more creative, legal and institutional solution or opportunity. The law *and* the long-term solution are both primary issues. The purpose of the Leading Lawyer's long-range focus is to 1) analyze legal issues, 2) solve existing problems and any foreseeable problems, and 3) to look beyond the immediate issues and seek institutional improvement and positive change. To accomplish this, the Leading Lawyer uses a well-developed analytical thinking process and a creative problem-solving methodology.

In developing these ideas, this chapter examines analytical and creative thinking processes and outlines the key steps one must implement to develop creative and problem-solving skills. We will explore the common characteristics of creative leaders and discuss traditional notions of creativity to dispel myths and false assumptions that impede the development of creative and entrepreneurial skills.

1. Analytical and Creative Approaches

a. Analytical Thinking

The analytical process that we use as lawyers is similar to what scientists, mathematicians, and engineers use. The scientific or analytical method, generally speaking, refers to the study of something by taking it apart. This approach became prominent about 400 years ago with the rise of rationality and science, Cartesian philosophy, Copernican astronomy, and Newtonian physics. It is an effective system for evaluating many problems and uses the following steps: define and formulate the problem; gather data; develop models of the data with well-established empirical techniques; explore alternatives; and reach a conclusion. It is based on gathering observable data and subjecting it to the principles of reason. The scientific method is taught as a sequential procedure that analyzes data, forms hypothesis, and employs deductive reasoning.[1]

The principles behind the legal analysis reflect the scientific method. We are taught to analyze a case by carefully dissecting its parts, determining its holding, and then applying the rule to a new set of facts. We analyze statutes by looking at each section, each sentence, and each carefully chosen word. In its simple form, our legal analysis follows the famous acronym that guides our basic legal analysis: IRAC—Issue, Rule, Analysis, and Conclusion.

Analytical thinking is very useful in systems analysis and for deductive reasoning based on unchanging scientific and mathematical rules. It is also effective in the interpretation of case and statutory law, as well as the many areas of legal discourse. However, it has limitations in effectively dealing with unstructured, elusive, and ambiguous issues.[2] The problems we encounter as lawyers involve many unquantifiable issues that make it difficult to rely solely upon the analytic approach. Individuals who are rational, irrational, and emotional can all be involved in the same situation and the effect of human interaction is difficult to calculate. Hard data is often inadequate and difficult to quantify; facts are usually in the grey zone of the law, which is why attorneys are needed to advocate an interpretation that is favorable to their client. Creative problem-solving is often the best way to approach such ambiguity.

b. Creative Thinking and Problem Solving

Creativity is a mental process that generates new ideas, concepts, or associations. This process, in a legal context, seeks to improve a situation for someone or their organization, something that is emphasized far less under an analytical approach, if at all. Instead of only looking backward at data or case law, the Leading Lawyer also looks to the future to define a more desirable legal and human situation, in addition to solving the existing problem. Leading Lawyers ask broad questions, are open to new concepts, and are nonjudgmental when it comes to new ideas. They have strong industry information and are curious about their clients' business. They are experts in their legal fields, have broad-based knowledge, and *always* seek cost-effective solutions to problems. Lawyers who lead start with an end in mind; from the onset of an assignment through its conclusion, they constantly look for previously unanticipated solutions or an unexpected opportunity. In short, a Leading Lawyer conjures up a better vision for the future.

In his book about negotiations, *Winning with Integrity*, sports attorney Leigh Steinberg addresses the importance of thinking creatively for the future:

to negotiate effectively for himself or a client, one must not only understand where a company is, but comprehend what that company, its product, and its industry can become.[3] Part of what you can offer in the negotiating context is a new vision of how the company's product might be packaged, marketed, and applied, and how you and your client can contribute to these new directions.[4]

As one example, Kordell Stewart's role in the Pittsburgh Steelers organization was *not* clear when he was drafted as a rookie in 1995. Several teams were interested in Stewart and tested him in a variety of positions—safety, running back, wide receiver and, of course, quarterback, the position he played at the University of Colorado and desperately wanted to keep. Given his unusual array of skills, Steinberg believed that Stewart could convince the team to re-shape the position to suit his abilities.[5] Steinberg and his client were able to describe and implement a different way in which Stewart could run the offense than had ever been done by the Steelers using Stewart's speed, running and throwing abilities. The negotiation was successful in giving the Steelers a vision of a new and more successful team. Stewart helped lead the Steelers to the Super Bowl a year later (though losing to the Cowboys). As Steinberg succinctly wrote: envision where your clients' industry is headed. Envision new outlets for and applications of the services or products you have to offer. When shaping your negotiating strategy, envision your client's growth.[6]

In Chapter Two, we talked about Big "L" Leadership and small "l" leadership. As we know, there are many people that have the responsibility of Big "L" leadership. In law firms, these include the management team and managing partner; in corporations it is the general counsel. While the majority of us spend our time in the small "l" leadership world, even this kind of leadership requires us to look forward and facilitate improvements; it means that we expect forward thinking from ourselves and all of our employees (remember the stock options are in Column B). Similar to the two scales of leadership, there is Big "V" Vision for the top-level leaders and small "v" vision in which everyone can participate and is grounded in creative thinking and problem solving.

Creativity has many definitions. One view holds that, in the broadest perspective, "creativity enables us to make something new and hitherto unimagined."[7] It involves the unexpected, the new, and the surprising.[8] In the context of entrepreneurship, creativity leads to the development of innovative products, services and processes that replace traditional or outdated versions.[9] In law, creativity moves lawyers from simple analysis to innovative problem-solving, providing the client with short-term legal solutions and helping them create long-term improvements. It is important to keep in mind that eventually, all of our clients will come to expect organizational improvements through creative problem-solving, in addition to traditional legal guidance and analysis. Leading Lawyers think like entrepreneurs when the time is right.

Peter Drucker, the father of modern business thinking, says that the heart of the entrepreneurial experience is innovation: the process that creates purposeful, focused, and positive change in an organization.[10] Another scholar views creativity as "a process of developing novel and useful ideas, whether an incremental improvement or a world-changing breakthrough; encompass[ing] a repeated cycle of divergence and convergence–to first create a rich diversity of options and then to agree on the best ideas to implement."[11] It is clear that Drucker would agree that creativity is a simple idea that emerges in common situations. Lawyers often have the opportunity to think creatively for their work, and a Leading Lawyer will recognize and seize those opportunities as they arise.

Creativity rarely occurs in isolation—it needs other people's minds, ideas, and inventions.[12] A Leading Lawyer must invoke creative thinking and overcome our general resistance to change. For the purpose of our endeavors as lawyers, we need to focus on service breakthroughs and efficiencies for our clients. How does one do this? Drucker suggests that *some* innovations spring from a flash of genius. However, *most* innovations, and usually the most successful ones, stem from a conscious search for creative opportunities and solutions. In other words, one has to *look* for opportunities and solutions; *create* the environment to find them; *develop* the process to discover them, and *implement* the solutions.[13] This is not a traditional legal process, but a creative, solution-oriented, and brainstorming method. Tom Kelly of IDEO (one of America's leading design firms) has learned that:

> [t]he problem with brainstorming is that everyone thinks
> [he or she] already do[es] it... Many business people treat
> brainstorming as a checkbox, a threshold... [T]hey overlook
> the possibility that brainstorming can be a skill, an art, more
> like playing the piano than tying your shoes. You're always
> learning and can get continuously better.... I believe you can
> deliver more value, create more energy, and foster more innovation through better brainstorming. For one thing, you
> could brainstorm more often, weaving it into the cultural

> *fabric of your organization... Brainstorming is practically a*
> *religion at IDEO ... brainstorming as a tool—as a skill—is*
> *taken quite seriously.*[14]

Leading Lawyers incorporate such creative thinking into their approach to each new challenge.

Also, the most effective lawyers always place an issue into its larger context. They understand the relationship between efficient action on the immediate problem and the potential for positive change on a grander scale. The Leading Lawyer's depth of insight is most clearly demonstrated in a story about three stone masons who were asked what they were doing. The first responded that he was stacking rocks. The second said he was making a wall. The third said he was building a cathedral. We, and our clients, are not always in the business of building cathedrals, but the Leading Lawyer has the blueprints in mind.

2. Creative Thinking and Problem Solving for Lawyers: Small "v" Vision

a. The Five Basic Steps for Leading Lawyers

Leading Lawyers know when to switch from purely analytical thinking to creative problem-solving, and how to effectively combine the two approaches. They understand that there is a time for legal analysis and tactical decision-making and a time for inquiry into wider opportunity and client solutions. While not all lawyers will become experts in innovation, they can learn to look at situations broadly and to investigate and assess the ever-expanding organizational issues of our clients. According to Peter Drucker, the leader of the past may have known how to answer, but the leader of the future will know how to ask.[15]

Leaders who display creative thinking, problem-solving, and entrepreneurial skills generally go through the five stages in a creative process:[16]

1. Identify the problems and opportunities

2. Generate many ideas

3. Prioritize, synthesize, and improve the ideas

4. Judge the best solution

5. Implement the best solution

i. *Identify the Problems and Opportunities*

Lawyers are presented with a host of issues, ranging from family law to mergers and acquisitions. The issue identification stage deals with discovery of the problem and the discovery of potential opportunities.[17] The Leading Lawyer solves not just the immediate problem, *but provides solutions for the problem after that as well.*

In *Breakthrough Thinking*, authors Nadler and Hibino outline some questions to ask—those that expand the investigation, not turn it inward as one might when relying exclusively on analytical thinking. Don't simply ask, "What's wrong here?" Instead ask, "What are you trying to accomplish? What are we trying to do? What are the purposes and needs of the client and their customers?" It is best to expand the investigation to examine the broader purpose and larger issues. Develop a picture of the array of small to larger issues and needs.[18]

Leading Lawyer Larry Sonsini observed that:

> *Clients often want the legal answer, but the legal answer is not the only point. It is important to keep things in perspective and in balance. Don't lose sight of the main thing. As one client, Jim Barksdale, whom I enjoyed working with when he was running Netscape, used to say, "the main thing is to be sure that the main thing, is the main thing." And I've always remembered that, because it encapsulated the way I have often approached my problems; the first question I try to ascertain is not what the legal answer is, but are we focusing on the right question, before we start answering?*[19]

As Sonsini suggests, Leading Lawyers go beyond legal analysis to participate in and direct the process of problem-solving. The most important concept in defining an issue is that solving the initial problem or dispute is invariably only the beginning. A great many more concerns, problems, and opportunities emerge with careful investigation and scrutiny.[20] The Leading Lawyer expands his thinking beyond the most immediate and obvious problem and thinks in broader terms of what the client really wants to accomplish.

It is part of our job to educate our clients and help them avoid repeating past mistakes. In return, our clients can show us how to best implement a solution within the organization, how to identify their needs, and assist them in pursuing their projects, business objectives, and cases. They need to participate in this process with us as partners. Before we try to win a case, we must understand what our clients consider a "win," what that win will cost, accomplish, and mean in the long run, and understand any alternatives. We should seek to know who our opponents are and how they can best be approached. Lawyers must make sure to get input on all these criteria from the client at each stage of the case or project; they must engage in a mutual decision-making process, and the criteria should be framed in terms of client input.

ii. Generate Many Ideas

In the preparation stage, one recognizes that creativity "does not come from out of the blue" but "springs from deep wells of expertise."[21] Research shows that the most creative people have a towering command of a given discipline, developed over many years. However, creative groups also need "beginners' minds"—newcomers to the field who bring fresh perspective and ask good questions.[22] The creative attorney will recall and collect information that is relevant, dreaming up a myriad of alternatives without prematurely refining, evaluating, or rejecting them.[23] Leading Lawyers also make sure that encouraging ideas is a group project, and create situations conducive to generating those ideas. Composing groups with newcomers and experts, as well as people with varied styles of insight, is extremely important for the creative leader.[24]

Ideas spring from diversity—of working and thinking styles, professional and personal experiences, education, and culture—within the group itself.[25] Thus, the generation of ideas or brainstorming is the most dynamic and social phase of the creative process.[26] Leading Lawyers know that they must conceive ideas with the help of their peers, teams, and clients. With few rules to constrain the endeavor, brainstorming is easy to learn.

a. Brainstorming

The general rules of brainstorming are easy to learn and perform in both a casual and formal way. *First*, generate as many solutions as possible. Ask questions that stimulate ideas, such as: "what would be the ideal solution? What are our clients' businesses and does this legal problem affect them? What can we do to solve this issue and improve their businesses?" You can enlarge your pool of ideas by being more inclusive in your approach. Encourage other attorneys to become involved in your case strategies.

Second, encourage all ideas, even the crazy ones, and allow freewheeling. Lawyers may be a bit embarrassed in this stage—we don't want to look foolish—but try stretching the limits with your ideas, or invite someone (perhaps someone other than a lawyer) to a session to help you. Many innovative ideas are never vocalized because of inhibitions and social constraints. Involve employees and constituents because, when involved, they are usually at their most productive. Collaboration inspires not just loyalty and dedication, but creativity. When people are given access to information and know their ideas will be respectfully considered and implemented when appropriate, they become part of a highly motivated team. Contrary to what some leaders assume, the more creative autonomy you give others the more willing they will typically become to contribute to the collective effort. Leading Lawyers know that the best ideas can emerge only after all ideas have been explored.

Third, build on the ideas of others; let one concept lead to another. Have a meeting with your clients to ask questions, explore options and possible outcomes. Clients can provide you with insights about their issues and problems which can also help you determine what legal services they need so you can proactively make your firm stand out in those business fields. Also, taking ideas from one business sector to another can be extremely effective. Rather than hunker down conservatively, challenge yourself and your team to learn about the industries in which you find yourselves, as well as industries outside your typical client base.

Fourth, criticism is not allowed; do not denigrate the ideas of others during a brainstorming session. Many brilliant ideas and strategies sounded ridiculous, unworkable, foolhardy, or bizarre before they were successfully implemented. A creative leader avoids asking disempowering or negative questions, e.g., those that assume or expect a preordained answer, response or strategy, or that make people defensive. Pronouncements do not facilitate innovative thinking; questions tend to lead to breakthroughs in productivity. Questions that presuppose blame, shut down free discourse, or prematurely reject possibilities accomplish the opposite of what you want: to create an open atmosphere of dialogue, where new ideas, not personalities, compete and emerge at the forefront.

How does one apply such brainstorming skills in difficult business, litigation, or policy contexts? Supreme Court Justice Thurgood Marshall's handling of the case *Brown v. Board of Education* provides an excellent example of leadership that combines the many attributes of a Leading Lawyer but highlights the need for creative thinking and problem-solving. The civil rights leader marshaled brilliant strategic insights, creative thinking and moral courage, personal innovation, and team-building skills to effect dramatic social transformation. Though dealing with highly charged and difficult racial and legal issues, Marshall used the creative process effectively.

> *Marshall was full of excitement and anticipation when he called a conference of attorneys from across the country to meet in New York. He was looking for a way to make the leap from desegregating graduate level schools to integrating all public schools. The meeting attracted wide attention...Jimmy Hicks of the Afro-American quoted Marshall as saying that the lawyers had mapped out plans to "wipe out all phases of segregation in education from professional school to kindergarten."[27]*

Marshall used this meeting to listen to others. He was never quick to judge or implement a plan, and always let those around him elaborate on the strongest arguments for all sides before beginning to solidify, or voice, his own opinion. In specific terms, Marshall and the NAACP had to strategize about whether to take the more moderate course of trying to ensure that racially "separate" schools were genuinely equal, or to radically challenge the entire notion of segregation itself. He listened to all sides:

> *At the New York meeting the voice most strongly pressing for the direct attack belonged to Spottswood Robinson. The Richmond lawyer, revered for his photographic memory and precise legal mind wanted the NAACP to be more aggressive. When they sat down at the meeting, Marshall began by expressing doubts about a strategy of asking the courts to rule that segregation was unconstitutional. This eventually goaded*

the gentlemanly Robinson into forcefully making the case for a direct attack. It also gave Marshall a chance to listen to the best arguments Robinson and the other lawyers could make for a court to disregard the Plessy decision and declare school segregation unconstitutional.

Other than smoking his cigarette and sometimes smiling, Marshall kept quiet as Robinson led the discussion of the new strategy. It was typical Marshall to let the arguments rage while he soaked in all sides to the debate.[28]

Marshall did not reach his decision or choose his tactic alone. He did not endorse the accepted position of trying to gain incremental equality or further piecemeal advances. After meeting with lawyers, judges, and colleagues, Marshall became convinced that the time had come when more comprehensive reform was not only possible, but necessary. With help, he developed a strategy for positive change.

On a much more conventional level, here is how it used to happen in my old law firm. Early in my career I worked for a fine lawyer named Randy Willoughby. As with many of the lawyers at Hoge Fenton Jones & Appel, Inc., he was a top-notch litigator and legal analyst. However, he was also a creative Leading Lawyer who used a simple technique to bring his partners and associates together for brainstorming opportunities with the help of two key players, his refrigerator and a great office administrator named Bob Bresacher who was kind enough to keep the refrigerator filled with a few refreshments. Usually by the end of the week, we gathered for a social meeting in Randy's office.

The meetings generated great ideas. Randy, as well as my other friends—such as Mark Davis, Alex Stuart, Brad Bening, and Peter Kirwan —would talk about their cases, the clients' problems, and legal and business solutions. The sessions were social as well as insightful. Everyone, from partners to young associates, was invited for refreshments and conversation. As I look back at it, Randy, who would "hold court" by asking questions and sparking discussions with a glass of wine in hand, was providing a great service to us all as well as to our clients. We were all involved in generating and evaluating ideas and solutions. Everyone was welcomed and participated in the conversation. Some of the best ideas I had as an attorney sprang from these informal meetings.

For example, as a young lawyer, I received a bit of help in one of these meetings when one of my colleagues simply said, "Buy the houses back." In representing contractors and developers, lawsuits were often filed for problems and defects in construction. Construction cases have a tendency to get expensive, and both sides spend excessively on attorney's and expert's fees. Furthermore, an insurance carrier is often involved on behalf of the builder, which effectively creates a second level of complexity. In one particular housing development that my client built, a series of alleged construction problems arose that were, at the very least, easily addressed. However, the plaintiff's attorney was pressing us for excessive repairs and future damages and claims because of the alleged problems and refused to let my client control the repairs. As a result of a simple, and perhaps obvious, suggestion in one of our "meetings," we outlined the way in which it would be better to repurchase the houses, repair, and resell them. I worked with the insurance carrier to fund a settlement and the builder agreed to repurchase the homes for the fair market value without the defects. The builder subsequently repaired the houses, disclosed all the issues, and provided a warranty to the new buyers. The houses were resold and the builder actually made a small profit. Again, this is not an overwhelmingly brilliant solution, but it is entrepreneurial in design and outlook. This idea was generated as a simple result of talking as a group with diverse experience and insight and being creative about our cases. I know we might try to take the creative approach for some of our cases and projects but my research shows that Leading Lawyers incorporate this creative process into most, if not *all*, of their activities.

iii. Idea Evaluation

A lawyer must evaluate issues from a creative perspective as well as the traditional legal point of view. Most often, in a legal setting this process seems to take place on an individual basis. However, a Leading Lawyer does not fail to acknowledge the benefit of including a diverse group in the evaluation process. Leading Lawyers recognize that a collaborative effort can perform this function more effectively and efficiently.

First, after you have generated a list of options, focus on those ideas of the highest quality. Take your selected ideas and work to make them more practical. Then synthesize those ideas in order to obtain more complete solutions. All the while, continue to look for great solutions.[29] Warren Bennis gives an example in one of his columns. He reports that "[a]fter the members of the

GE board had agreed to name Jeff Immelt to succeed Jack Welch...the board took three weeks to let the decision sit before the official vote was taken and an announcement made. Leaders must always be certain they are accessing the full spectrum of data and opinion."[30] The process includes looking at the immediate problem and the ideas that were generated, and then evaluating the variety of issues that could arise in the future. Consider the positive and negative implications of your potential solutions. Think like a chess player, as Anna Muoio suggests in her article "All the Right Moves," in which expert chess strategist Bruce Pandolfini describes the critical evaluation stage in chess:

> *The issue isn't how far ahead great players think, but how they think in the moment. Great players consider their next move without playing it—and then consider their opponent's response to that move...*

> *Most players look for a "bit": They see a good move, and they make it. That's an error. You should never play the first good move that comes into your head. Put that move on your list, and ask yourself if an even better move [is available]. "If you see a good idea, look for a better one"—that's my motto. Good thinking is a matter of making comparisons...*[31]

Leading Lawyers inspire others to solve bigger and more complex problems creatively by asking questions instead of judging. Individuals need time and space to reflect on solutions or considerations that may not be immediately apparent.[32] While the information is simmering, it is being arranged into meaningful new patterns.[33] One of the important skills of creativity, and of leadership in general, is knowing when to take time for such reflection.[34] Leading Lawyers reflect and anticipate—contemplating solutions and always looking for better ones:

> *The ultimate solutions to problems are rational; the process for thinking of fresh solutions is not. Right-brain thinking processes allow the mind to diverge from the current point of understanding—the problem. Many great thinkers get as far away from the problem as possible to allow true breakthroughs to happen. Da Vinci, Einstein, Galileo, and Pinkerton would remove their task from their thoughts and*

> *playfully generate seemingly irrelevant material [that] they*
> *would connect back to their problem. This would allow them*
> *to experiment with fresh ideas and develop fresh solutions.*[35]

Idea evaluation requires you to assess the directions, strategy, or solutions from the rich diversity of options assembled.[36] Unfortunately, individuals too often seek quick closure with a solution that may preclude more effective alternatives.[37] Skillful leaders balance the need for a wide variety of options with the need for closure.[38] It is useful to continually analyze the situation. As Marshall did in the case of *Brown v. Board of Education*, it is best to work with others to further develop the issue and your ideas before beginning your course of action.

In evaluating the legal position in *Brown*, Marshall and his colleagues worked as a group to strategize and evaluate the best ideas and most effective strategies. A colleague suggested taking the novel approach of using extra-legal sociological data, showing that segregated schools demonstrably affected the self-esteem of black children, to bolster their arguments in court. Studies showed that black children consistently identified white dolls as desirable and virtuous, and black dolls as undesirable and inferior:

> *When black children were presented with black and white*
> *dolls, they almost always said the white dolls were prettier,*
> *smarter, and better at everything they did.*

> *When Carter presented the idea of using (this) research*
> *to the lawyers at the NAACP, there was little support. Spott-*
> *swood Robinson, for example, thought it was crazy and in-*
> *sulting to try to persuade a court of law with examples of*
> *crying children and their dolls. But Marshall, in a surprise to*
> *his colleagues, sided with Carter. He stood up and said if the*
> *time has come for a direct challenge to segregation, then there*
> *was no reason not to use sociology, psychology, or anything*
> *else if it might help to win the case.*[39]

Despite numerous setbacks, including lower court decisions in which clearly biased judges refused to consider any empirical data, Marshall realized he had to take segregation head-on in the Supreme Court, and call for its complete reversal. Marshall decided that they should use all available data and disciplines to document the debilitating effects of educational discrimination and contest segregation in elementary and secondary schools. Risking the loss of many gains made to implement equal education under the segregationist system, Marshall persevered to dismantle it entirely.[40]

By listening to those around him, Marshall came up with a strategy that took into account the social and political implications of his case. This extended far beyond the group's preliminary approach; Marshall viewed his task not exclusively in the context of law, but history, social change, regional cultures, group behavior, psychology, anthropology, and politics. An emblematic Leading Lawyer, Marshall knew when to be patient in strategic terms, but also when to risk approaches that had yet to be validated under familiar legal paradigms. This approach was the direct result of a creative process and evaluation of the multiplicity of ideas generated by many people, which took into account information far beyond customary legal considerations.

iv. Analyze the Options and Decide

Lawyers at this stage of the process find themselves in familiar territory. This step uses the imagination, but also focuses on analytical and critical thinking skills. Reflect upon the information, evidence, and reasoning, and form judgments about the alternatives. Mayor Guiliani said about this phase, that:

> *Making the right choices is the most important part of leadership. Every other element–from developing and communicating ideas to surrounding oneself with great people –relies on making good decisions... Faced with any important decision, I always envision how each alternative will play out before I make it. During this process, I am not afraid to change my mind a few times. Many are tempted to decide an issue simply to end the discomfort of the decision. However, the longer you have to make a decision, the more mature and well-reasoned that decision should be.*[41]

The judgment stage occurs when the individual sets out to prove that their creative solution has merit.[42] Verification procedures include gathering supporting evidence, using logical persuasion, and experimenting with new ideas.[43] This stage also requires a good deal of contextual thinking and forethought;

it is largely situational. Timing is important. Ask yourself, does the situation require, or would it benefit from, a quick decision, or do you have the time to evaluate the options gradually, and give each alternative a full vetting?

There are many different models, including Pareto analysis, paired comparison analysis, and decision trees that allow the best decision makers to develop a list of criteria, goals, and priorities with their clients. They then go through a series of exercises. They compare the options to the list of criteria, and prioritize them or assign a score, a priority number, or value to each option. Then, they evaluate the options by projecting likely outcomes. You can do this with a sophisticated decision tree analysis or something less formal. Next, they list the advantages and disadvantages of each option. Lastly, the team uses advocacy and inquiry to evaluate the best and the weakest arguments, and the reasons behind their choices. Lawyers have a tendency to use this method exclusively without the weighing and balancing. Often the most senior or experienced advocate wins the day, which does not always produce the best result. It might help to use a related exercise and that is to consider how a judge would see the issue and try to solve the problem, rather than arguing a position. Perhaps an even more useful exercise is to think like one's client. By placing oneself in the client's position and even directly asking the client for input, an attorney can learn as much crucial information about a case as he might by reading many treatises on the relevant subject matter. Every good lawyer will know the contours of the law; Leading Lawyers will understand how to use the law, creative thinking, and problem-solving to best serve the motivations and needs of their clients as well.

Once you have synthesized the evaluations, making a clear decision is crucial. Arthur Martinez, the former CEO of Sears, director of PepsiCo and Saks 5th Ave., and author of *The Hard Road to the Softer Side*, stresses the importance of being flexible and open-minded, but also decisive, in approaching new situations:

> *The issue for most people in leadership positions is to seize that moment and to act on it—as opposed to shutting it down and saying, "I need more data, more analysis, more time, more certainty." At some point, clarity develops, and a bright light shines through. The challenge for you as a leader is to know when that happens and act on your best instinct*

and judgment—but be sure to act as opposed to reflect and ponder...

I always told myself and my team that whatever got us here to where we are now, by definition, is insufficient to get us where we need to go. Returning to old play books, old approaches to problems and old styles of leading people are likely to fail today. So, be willing to throw out the old play book and write a new one.[44]

Once a clear decision has been made, a Leading Lawyer will facilitate its implementation.

v. Implementation.

Implementation takes teamwork, vision, goal setting, and a host of additional skill sets that are outlined in other sections. A good decision needs group acceptance. You and your client need to come to a joint decision. Work with your client, team members, and other stakeholders so that everyone understands and believes in the approach. A work plan needs to be developed and goals and timelines met. The process of implementation is difficult and usually involves deferred gratification, not instant success. An honest assessment of how long a project will need to reach fruition greatly increases your chances of successfully carrying your strategy through to the desired outcome. A Leading Lawyer recognizes that successful implementations of even the best ideas require the support of those involved; they require a vision for the future.

Now that we have discussed the ways in which lawyers can design, vet, and implement their small "v" vision, we can examine the themes of Big "V" Vision and explore how those too may be applicable in more common situations and by Leading Lawyers at all levels of an organization.

3. Big "V" Vision

The skill of Big "V" Vision is one that managing partners and general counsel typically display as well as many other top leaders within an organization. Big "V" Vision is also a concept slightly beyond the scope of this book and so I offer only a brief overview of the themes and for you to consider how they might translate to all levels of an organization. All the best books on leadership discuss this level of Vision and I would refer you to such books such as Posner and Kouzes' *The Leadership Challenge, Good to Great* by Jim Collins, and *The Extraordinary Leader* by Zenger and Folkman. For our more general purposes, the concept of Vision can be broken down in to several distinct themes. These concepts are used generally in larger organizations and campaigns, but the themes can also be applied successfully in smaller groups and projects.

First and foremost, one must define a shared vision and seek to *find a common ground*. It is important to create a common purpose with your constituents on which you will base your vision. Leaders forge a unity of purpose by showing their constituents how the vision can meet their needs and serve a common good.[45] With an increase in diversity, both in workforce and customers, and with the influence of the Internet, your ability to enlist people [in your vision] depends on how effective you are at determining the "ties that bind."[46] Frame your vision in a way that appeals to your audience. Kouzes and Posner believe that "[t]he best way to get to know what other people want is to sit down and talk with them on their turf."[47] They assert that a leader must fully understand the needs and interests of the people involved in the success of the vision and suggest that a complete understanding requires the leader to walk in the shoes of those who they seek to lead. "No matter how grand the dream of an individual visionary, if others don't see in it the possibility of realizing their own hopes and desires, they won't follow. Leaders must show other how they, too, will be served by the long-term vision of the future, how their specific needs can be satisfied."[48]

Second, one must develop a solution or vision for your project or organization that is *clear and compelling*. You should know where you want to go before you expect people to follow your vision or help implement your solution. It is largely held that a compelling vision will unleash energy and potential.[49] In *Leading for a Lifetime*, they state that you must communicate the "urgency and superiority" of your vision or solution in a way that will "galvanize and inspire others."[50] In *Lincoln on Leadership,* Donald Phillips makes the point that:

> *People must accept and implement [the vision] whole-heartedly and without reservation. When this is achieved, it is always done with enthusiasm, commitment, and pride...If the*

*working troops understand what is expected of them, what the
organization is trying to accomplish, then it becomes possible
to make important decision on lower levels, thereby creating a
climate in which results and progress continually occur.*[51]

A vision that can be stated clearly, concisely, and provide people with a vivid
picture of what the future could be like, is a vision more likely to be brought
to fruition and effect a positive change.

Third, leaders must *fully commit* to their vision and be able to explain why
others should care as well. You must personally believe in something before
you can create a climate of purpose. In order to inspire others, you have to be
inspired.[52] External motivation is more likely to create conditions of compliance or defiance; self-motivation produces far superior results people who are
self-motivated will keep working toward a result even if there's no reward, but
people who are externally controlled are likely to stop trying once the rewards
or punishments are removed.[53] People want leaders with enthusiasm, energy,
and a positive attitude. They want to believe that they will contribute to an
invigorating journey.[54]

Fourth, "work has become a place where people pursue meaning and iden-
tity."[55] Leading Lawyers are able to elicit and mobilize this human need by
communicating the meaning and significance of their vision so that people
understand and take ownership of their individual role in pursuing the goal.
"What matters isn't the eloquence of the speech but the appeal of the message
to the audience. For that appeal to exist, leaders have to understand other's
dreams, and they have to find common ground on which to build a shared
dream."[56] Progress toward a shared vision should bring meaning to the work,
be consistent with shared values, and serve participants' interests. In order to
effect positive change at an organizational level, inevitably it will require sacrifice. Demonstrate why the vision is worthy of such sacrifice and clearly identify
the benefits that the stakeholders will enjoy in exchange for their support.

Fifth, Big "V" Vision also requires a leader with emotional intelligence
that *enables and inspires* their constituents and workforce. Leaders facilitate
an environment that will allow people to exceed their previous best performance.[57] When leaders clearly communicate a shared vision of an organization, they ennoble those who work on its behalf and elevate the human spirit.[58]
If a leader can put everyone on a "dynamic and forceful upward spiral of

action and commitment"[59] they will realize steadier and greater progress than by simply throwing money at the problem. Leading Lawyers break the journey down into measurable goals and milestones, demonstrating how progress can be made incrementally[60] with team work and ingenuity. A true Leading Lawyer will abandon their ego in order to "unleash the talents of others"[61] in an effort to further the common purpose.

Finally, a leader should *continually refresh and reinforce* their vision with vitality and excitement about progress made or lessons learned from setbacks. "Repeating and renewing [the] vision so that it would not diminish in meaning" is the process of renewal that [is], in effect, the greatest form of motivation. Over time, as values decay and incentives dwindle, leaders must constantly provide a rejuvenating process."[62] Success, in an ever-increasingly aggressive market, takes continuous long-term vision for a company to remain innovative and competitive.[63] Seeing a vision through to reality often requires both persistence and collaboration.[64] The process of renewal releases the critical human talent and energy that is necessary to ensure success.[65]

The story of how William Loris helped found the International Development Law Organization (IDLO) in order to help underdeveloped countries draft and establish laws and operate peacefully within the rule of law, provides a great example of how Big "V" Vision can work. Armed with his master's and law degree, and with very little legal experience, Loris took his first job working for the State Department in the U.S. Agency for International Development. His first post was in Abidjan in West Africa when he was 27 years old, helping to solve legal and practical problems in many African villages. Due to severe lack of resources, his boss was unable to spare the time necessary to train Loris, so he was left to rely on his seemingly unrelated educational background and basic common sense. As he dove into his responsibilities of making policy decisions on how African villages and people should solve their problems and structure their laws, Loris came to realize that Africans should be making these decisions themselves; it was the African lawyers who should have been involved.

He began to develop his vision to help bring the rule of law to more underdeveloped countries. Loris wanted to get the local citizens, attorneys, and judges involved in working out their country's own problems and solutions. However, Loris knew that unfortunately, many of the lawyers and citizens in the developing world were ill equipped to handle such an undertaking. So, while on a fishing trip with his colleague, Michael Hager, Loris pitched his idea to train lawyers and judges and get them involved in creating the new infrastructure for their countries. In brainstorming how this could be best accomplished, they set up an expert training and education symposium with people they knew to be experts in this field. During and after the meeting, they received many papers about teaching methodology, advice as to where they could find participants, and how best to approach the countries where each expert had contacts. Loris and Hager also wrote a paper and solicited people all over the world who might be interested and willing to help them accomplish their task.

They were surprised by the overwhelmingly positive response to their request for help and, in time, added new members with diverse backgrounds and varying expertise to their team. Together, they founded the IDLO which provides lawyers and judges with training so that they could take control of their own destinies and develop the codes, rules, and the procedures of law in their developing countries. Through their repeated successes, the IDLO has become a major player with an international development agenda and leads some of the world's biggest legal reform projects. For example, they were the first agency to establish training and assistance in Afghanistan to lawyers and judges establishing the rule of law after the fall of the Taliban.

Loris and the IDLO seek to further the organization's goals by empowering its nearly 17,000 alumni (people who have been educated and trained by the IDLO) to facilitate, create, and eventually lead the process of instituting the rule of law in their home countries. In my interview with Loris, he described how the organization encourages its members to take the lead on projects. Because the IDLO thus empowers its members, they have managed to legally establish themselves into foundations in 42 countries. Loris stresses the need to effectively communicate the shared vision and to stand aside and allow others the necessary freedoms to help accomplish the goal.

In order to fully invoke his idea to train lawyers and judges in the virtues of the rule of law, Loris developed a vision; found the common ground with those who wanted to be involved and clearly and compellingly communicated the vision. Loris demonstrated his complete dedication to the goal through his perseverance and was able to communicate the meaning and significance of his quest. Furthermore, he designed the IDLO protocol to enable and inspire its members to become a part of the process, and Loris continually refreshed and reinforced the vision by helping the organization to continually expand and ensure its ongoing success.

We cannot all be William Loris, general counsel or managing partner. Their level of authority and responsibility required them to operate with the techniques of Big "V" Vision on a near-daily basis in order to implement change on a larger stage than a majority of lawyers operate on. However, while Big "V" Vision is typically used by the Jack Welches, Rudy Guilianis, and managing partners, the complex skills and themes of Big "V" Vision can be applied successfully at more basic levels when you find yourself with a vision for positive change.

4. Overcoming Traditional Thinking, Myths, & False Assumptions

Many people believe that one is either born with or without the ability to think creatively. Furthermore, that those who were born creative will lose their natural creativity because of exposure to influences from home, school, work and culture.[66] We as lawyers suffer from this negative acculturation. The rigors of law school and the practice of law may hamper our motivation to be creative. However, there are several common myths that we can, and must learn to overcome in order to better tap into our creative sides.

Myth 1: *Creativity only comes from creative types.*

Research shows that anyone with normal intelligence is capable of performing creative work.[67] Creativity depends on a number of things: experience (including knowledge and technical skills); talent; an ability to think in new ways; and the discipline and strength to work through creative dry spells.[68] Intrinsic motivation is especially critical in that individuals who are interested and excited by their work are often more creative. Unfortunately, most individuals do not realize their creative potential because they work in an environment that suppresses intrinsic motivation.[69] Nadler and Hibino, experts who researched this issue, report that 5-8% of people are born with expert creative thinking abilities, and that 5-8% have no ability and will probably never improve.[70] The remaining 84-90% have innate creative abilities that can be honed with technique and practice. Lawyers have plenty of room for growth.

Myth 2: *Money motivates creativity.*

Research on creativity suggests that money isn't everything.[71] In a famous study conducted by one of the country's foremost explorers of business innovation, Teresa Amabile, participants were asked "To what extent were you motivated by rewards today?"[72] They often answered that the question wasn't relevant—they don't think about pay on a day-to-day basis.[73] Likewise, the handful of people who were spending a lot of time wondering about their bonuses were doing little creative thinking.[74]

The research shows that people put far more value on a work environment where creativity is supported, valued, and recognized.[75] People crave the opportunity to be engaged in their work and make real progress. Leading Lawyers must match individuals to work projects, not only on the basis of their experience, but their interests. Individuals are most creative when they care about their work and feel challenged.[76] If the challenge goes far beyond their skill level, they tend to get frustrated; if it is far below their skill level, they tend to get bored. Leaders must strike the right balance.[77]

Myth 3: *Time pressures fuel creativity.*

Amabile's study also compiled 12,000 daily journal entries from 238 people working on creative projects in seven different companies in the consumer products, high-tech, and chemical industries. The study showed that people often thought they were most creative when they were working under severe deadline pressures.[78] However, the 12,000 aggregate days of research showed the opposite: people were the least creative when they were pressed for time.[79] Their creativity decreased not only on that day, but the following two days. Time pressure stifles creativity because people cannot deeply engage with problems.[80] Creativity requires an incubation period for one to absorb a problem and let ideas bubble up.[81] Leading Lawyers know to discuss, creatively analyze and focus on issues with ample time to allow for brainstorming and change. They will discuss the problem and potential solutions long before the deadline.

Myth 4: *Fear forces breakthroughs.*

Many also believe that fear increases creativity. However, in Amabile's research, this was not established.[82] In her study, researchers coded all 12,000 journal entries for the degree of fear, anxiety, sadness, anger, joy, and love that people experienced on a given day.[83] They found that creativity is positively associated with joy and love, and negatively associated with anger, fear, and anxiety.[84] The entries show that people are happiest when they come up with a creative idea, but are more likely to have a breakthrough if they were happy the day before, creating a kind of "virtuous cycle."[85] When people are excited about their work, there is a greater chance that "they will make a cognitive association that incubates overnight and shows up as a creative idea the next day: one day's happiness often predicts the next day's creativity."[86] For lawyers, fear is often the result of being unprepared. Rudy Giuliani advises that it is with "relentless preparation"[87] that a lawyer dispels that fear and is able to think more clearly and creatively.

Myth 5: *Competition beats collaboration.*

Many believe that internal competition fosters innovation.[88] However, Amabile's study demonstrates that creativity dissipates when workers compete instead of collaborate.[89] The most creative teams shared and debated ideas. However, when people competed for recognition, they stopped sharing information.[90] When the workplace becomes more collaborative, it also becomes more creative: we can focus most of our attention on learning, action, and growth. As we work with others, we trust ourselves more—we take greater chances and risks, secure that our colleagues will support us.

Lawyers have particular hurdles to overcome in this area because we are socialized to be competitive. Law school emphasizes competition over collaboration at every level, and law professors often grade students using a zero sum model that precludes teamwork. Law school also tends to teach us to think within narrow paradigms, to regurgitate formulaic answers within an advocacy model that professors recognize and reward rather than to develop independent evaluations or creative solutions. Competition of course has its place—in sports, advocacy, and business for example—and can be a significant motivating factor. However, in law, one might argue that an undue emphasis on competition has led to a belief that no mutual gain is possible, and is a lack of social cohesion or social responsibility. This can result in a dysfunctional culture that values victory over mutual or team benefit. Here, the Leading Lawyer, when appropriate, sees not only the side he may have been putatively assigned to advocate, but also the larger picture. They seek to effect positive change for all of those involved as well as the best possible outcome for their client, and they will collaborate with team members and even opposing counsel to arrive at the best solution.

Myth 6: *There is only one right answer.*

The belief that only one correct answer exists is a serious barrier to creativity when dealing with other than purely mathematical problems.[91] Looking for alternatives is especially important when dealing with ideas.[92] However, "How do we know our answer is best if we have nothing to compare it with?"[93] Univocal thinking "freezes people into place and leads them to ignore data that supports other positions until change is forced upon them by failure or crisis."[94] Unless we are clear on our goals and the full range of options, we will likely precipitously choose an inchoate or inadequate solution. A Leading Lawyer recognizes that there can be more than one solution to most legal problems and their goal it to seek the best one.

Myth 7: *Analyze problems in isolation.*

Looking at a problem in isolation is a mental block.[95] Before an individual can find answers to a problem, he must find out if the problem is part of a larger issue.[96] The context is always relevant. Narrow points of view can impede creative thinking, and tend to impose the greatest limitations when individuals become experts in their fields.[97] Discussing issues with others often results in the most effective solutions. As Tom Kelly points out, brainstorming is "a persuasive cultural influence for making sure that individuals don't waste too much energy spinning their wheels on a tough problem when the collective wisdom of the team can get hem 'unstuck' in less than an hour."[98]

Myth 8: *Always follow the rules.*

Following rules mechanically is a form of autonomic behavior that requires wisdom to overcome.[99] A person must question existing constraints before they can create novel ideas.[100] When one does not question arbitrary or inherited criteria, an individual may miss opportunities for creative thinking and improvements.[101] Sometimes rules are followed long after the original reason for them has evaporated.[102] As Larry Sonsini put it, "one must always create different rules in a business negotiation,"[103] and as Elizabeth Cabraser rightly points out, "We have a common law system, so if you don't like the law, you get to go out and make some of your own."[104] Leading Lawyers often develop novel rules to fit new scenarios.

5. Conclusion

Leading Lawyers facilitate and encourage their teams to be creative. They are broad thinkers who help develop ideas and visions for themselves and others. Creative thinking enables Leading Lawyers to contribute novel insights that can open up new opportunities or alternatives for their client or organization. Although they often begin with legal analysis, they expand the process into one that creates solutions. Truly effective leaders are not overly constrained by analytical thinking and they work to cultivate and fully develop their creative, problem-solving, and entrepreneurial skills.

It must be acknowledged that there is an inherent difficulty in outlining these processes: prescribing rules for creativity (and leadership in general) suggests that there is a "correct" method. Innovators realize that many rules interfere with creativity more than they nurture it; that old rules often won't apply to new and different situations; and that leaders challenge rules as often as they formulate them. Leaders agree that vision and creative problem-solving is an *adaptive*, flexible process: a series of responsive approaches and perspectives, rather than an end point or series of fixed rules and methods. As with any skill, leadership and creativity is something that can be learned, and must be practiced, before successfully improvised.

Learning how to develop a vision, solve problems creatively, and become a successful leader is a process of understanding the needs of yourself, your clients, and your colleagues; it is developing the will and motivation to make improvements; it requires internalizing and practicing a variety leadership approaches; and promoting an attitude that prizes foresight, collaboration, and positive change. We can learn to practice law and we can learn to practice the creative thinking skills of leadership. Now, we turn to another important part of the leadership process: developing communication and persuasion skills.

Notes

1. Edward Lumsdaine and Martin Binks, Entrepreneurship, Creativity, and Effective Problem Solving, 62 (2005).

2. *Id.* at 63.

3. Leigh Steinberg and Michael D'Orso, *Winning With Integrity*, 59-60 Three Rivers Press (1998).

4. *Id.* at 60-61.

5. *Id.* at 57-59.

6. *Id.*

7. Lumsdaine and Binks, *supra* note 1, at 23.

8. *Id.*

9. *Id.*

10. Peter Drucker, *Classic Drucker*, 69 Harvard Business School Press (2006).

11. Frances Hesselbein and Rob Johnston, *On Creativity, Innovation, and Renewal*, 56 Jossey-Bass (2002).

12. *Id.* at 24.

13. Drucker, *supra* note 10 at 69-70.

14. Tom Kelly, *The Art of Innovation*, 55-56 Profile Books (2001).

15. Drucker, *supra* note 10 at 127-129.

16. Hesselbein and Johnston, *supra* note 11 at 56-57; Andrew DuBrin, *Leadership*, 326-27 Houghton & Mifflin (4th ed. 2004).

[17.] DuBrin, *supra* note 16 at 326-327.

[18.] Gerald Nadler and Shozo Hibino, *Breakthrough Thinking*, 10 Prima Publishing (2nd ed. 1994).

[19.] Interview with Larry Sonsini, August 2006.

[20.] Nadler and Hibino, *supra* note 18 at 129.

[21.] Hesselbein and Johnston, *supra* note 11 at 56.

[22.] *Id.*

[23.] *Id.*

[24.] *Id.*

[25.] Hesselbein and Johnston, *supra* note 11 at 57.

[26.] *Id.*

[27.] Juan Williams, *Thurgood Marshall*, 195 Times Books (1998).

[28.] *Id.* at 195-196.

[29.] Lumsdaine and Binks, *supra* note 1 at 80.

[30.] Warren Bennis,"What Do Leaders Know?", *Leadership Excellence Online*, *available at* http://www.leaderexcel.com/ (accessed August 2007)

[31.] Anna Muoio, "All the Right Moves", *Fast Company*, 24 (April 1999), *available at* http://www.fastcompany.com/magazine/24/chess.html.

[32.] Hesselbein and Johnston, *supra* note 11 at 57.

[33.] *Id.*

[34.] *Id.*

[35.] Joseph R. McKinney, "Prepared to Lead", *Leadership Excellence Online*, (December 2006), *available at* http://www.leaderexcel.com/.

[36.] Hesselbein and Johnston, *supra* note 11 at 57.

[37.] *Id.*

[38.] *Id.*

[39.] Williams, *supra* note 27 at 197.

[40.] Willaims, *supra* note 27 at 195-208.

[41.] Rudolph Guliani, *Leadership*, 122 Miramax Books (2002).

[42.] DuBrin, *supra* note 16 at 327.

[43.] *Id.* at 327.

[44.] Interview of Arthur Martinez in *Executive Excellence Online*, (February 2002), *available at* http://www.leaderexcel.com/.

[45.] James S. Kouzes and Barry Z. Posner, "Exemplary Vision", *Executive Excellence Online*, *available at* http://www.leaderexcel.com, (accessed August 2007).

46. James S. Kouzes and Barry Z. Posner, *The Leadership Challenge*, 161 Jossey-Bass (3rd ed. 2002).

47. *Id.*

48. *Id.* at 148.

49. Ken Blanchard and Jesse Stoner, "The Power of Vision", *Executive Excellence Online*, available at http://www.leaderexcel.com, (accessed August 2007).

50. Warren Bennis and Robert Thomas, *Leading for a Lifetime*, 134 Harvard Business School (2007).

51. Donald Phillips, *Lincoln on Leadership*, 164 Warner Books (1992).

52. Kouzes and Posner, *supra* note 46 at 112.

53. *Id.*

54. *Id.* at 157.

55. *Id.* at 152.

56. *Id.* at 148.

57. Kouzes and Posner, *supra* note 45.

58. Kouzes and Posner, *supra* note 46 at 152.

59. Phillips, *supra* note 51 at 168.

60. Kouzes and Posner, *supra* note 45.

61. Bennis and Thomas, *supra* note 50 at 139.

62. Phillips, *supra* note 51 at 166.

63. Tom Schmitt and Arnold Pearl, *Simple Solutions*, 129 John Wiley & Sons, Inc. (2007).

64. *Id.* at 131.

65. Phillips, *supra* note 51 at 168.

66. Lumsdaine and Binks, *supra* note 1 at 27.

67. Bill Breen, "The 6 Myths of Creativity", *Fast Company*, available at http://www.fastcompany.com/magazine/89/creativity.html (accessed October 5, 2006).

68. *Id.*

69. *Id.*

70. Nadler and Hibino, *supra* note 18 at xvi.

71. *Id.*

72. *Id.*

73. *Id.*

74. Breen, *supra* note 67.

75. *Id.*

76. *Id.*

77. *Id.*

78. *Id.*

79. *Id.*

80. *Id.*

81. *Id.*

82. *Id.*

83. *Id.*

84. *Id.*

85. *Id.*

86. Breen, *supra* note 67.

87. Interview with Rudy Giuliani, August 2008.

88. Breen, *supra* note 67.

89. *Id.*

90. *Id.*

91. Lumsdaine and Binks, *supra* note 1 at 28.

92. *Id.*

93. *Id.*

94. Jennifer James, *Thinking in the Future Tense: Leadership Skills for a New Age*, 198 Touchstone (1996).

95. *Id.*

96. *Id.*

97. *Id.*

98. Kelly, *supra* note 14 at 5.

99. Lumsdaine and Binks, *supra* note 1 at 28.

100. *Id.*

101. *Id.*

102. *Id.*

103. Interview with Larry Sonsini, August 2006.

104. Interview with Elizabeth Cabraser, August 2008.

CHAPTER SIX:
Effectively Communicate and Persuade

Lawyers are adept at communicating arguments by advocating for and articulating a position. However, not all lawyers are adept at the alternate forms of communication and persuasion, which might more effectively accomplish their goals. Our law schools teach oral and written advocacy, notably through class discussions, clinics, and moot-court programs because lawyers build careers, inside and outside the legal field, by facing situations that demand advocacy. However, in business, political, social, and legal arenas, as negotiators, creative problem-solvers, and deal-makers, Leading Lawyers develop and sharpen their ability to communicate and persuade in ways beyond advocacy.

I am not suggesting that we abandon our advocacy skills. Lawyers have consistently obtained results from communicating through advocacy in conventional legal settings and it can be a valuable form of persuasion used to sway those who determine disputes such as judges, arbitrators, lawyers, and many others who respond well to advocacy. However, as plenty of evidence will support, advocacy is often not the most effective method of persuasion. The adversarial underpinnings of our legal system are more conducive to conflict, even when it might be more useful to focus on the underlying needs of your client and the

"Communication is another element of leadership—leadership requires a tremendous amount of communication. And, there are many ways to communicate. You can communicate in writing or verbally and through action. We put a great degree of emphasis upon communication in all ways."

Larry Sonsini
Wilson, Sonsini,
Goodrich & Rosati

"It all culminates in communication, so without communication none of the other [leadership] principles mean anything... it's the one [skill] that makes the others work."

Mayor Rudy Giuliani
Former Mayor
of New York

other parties involved. Leading lawyers understand that in negotiating, solving problems, and brokering deals there will be a time to act competitively through advocacy but there is also a time when cooperative problem-solving and non-confrontational business communication will be more persuasive, and more effective, on a grander scale. Developing the skills of alternative communication and persuasion techniques, and knowing when and how to use them, is a skill which can be mastered. It does take insight, awareness, and even some courage to depart from the familiar set of expectations and familiarity of the adversarial system.

1. Laywers Are Great Advocates but Effective Communication Demands More

I have been involved in and studied negotiation, dispute resolution, and leadership for many years now and have found that, much of the time, clients need their lawyers to possess skill sets that include listening, developing a rational and emotional connection with their audience, and consensus-building. Yet the idea that lawyers can persuade using these techniques remains foreign to many of my lawyer friends. "Nothing like a great legal and rational argument," they say. However, the attempt to "win," an insistence on rigid goals, and an attempt to fix outcomes in advance lead to situations that can actually become counterproductive and escalate conflict.

Take a moment to consider the different audiences that a lawyer will address during the course of their career. Lawyers must communicate with bosses, peers, and subordinates within their organization. They interact with individual clients, as well as officers and directors representing both profit and nonprofit corporate clients. Solicitations must be made within, and to, client organizations. Lobbyists must influence legislators, regulators, and executives. Politicians must motivate voters, business interests, party groups, and an array of other constituencies. The goal of being persuasive in each communication to every audience requires a tailored approach, calling for awareness and understanding of the history, needs, and emotions of the people involved. Rational argumentation and rhetoric are useful, but they are only a few of the myriad of effective communication and persuasion styles.

For example, a study by Gary Yukl and J. Bruce Tracey investigated the effectiveness of a group of managers. A survey was conducted that included the manager's superiors, peers, and subordinates and focused on which communication tactics had the greatest and most positive impact. Yukl and Tracey's research, and the larger theory of which it is a part, shows there are many ways to persuade.[1] Nine communication approaches were identified for the participants:

1. Rational persuasion
2. Inspirational appeal
3. Consultation
4. Ingratiation
5. Exchange
6. Personal appeal
7. Coalition building
8. Legitimating
9. Pressure

According to Andrew DuBrin's precis of Yukl and Tracey's study, "noncoercive tactics that provide a rational and justifiable basis for change are more effective in gaining compliance than threats or manipulation."[2] The research found that the most effective forms of communication are rational persuasion, inspirational appeal, and consultation. The study concluded that of nine influence tactics identified, the least effective are pressure and explicit assertions of authority. Not only is coercion a poor way to persuade, it virtually never elicits genuine commitment. In fact, use of coercive tactics usually runs the risk of backlash, where employees, peers, and adversaries take the first opportunity to show their dissatisfaction and push back. People who have been manipulated, coerced, or "argued" into accepting positions may later either vote against or verbally undermine the position or project to express their disaffection, or even sabotage what they felt artificially compelled to support.[3] In "Harnessing the Science of Persuasion," psychology professor Robert Cialdini observed that when a commitment feels involuntary, even managers are unlikely to follow through.[4] People who have been manipulated, instead of persuaded, tend to abandon the initiative before completion, either because, deep down they expect or even want it to fail, or because they feel forced to endorse an endeavor they were neither invested in nor had a chance to influence.[5]

In contrast, true persuasion is not a form of control but an ongoing dialogue. The hard sell delivered once is never as effective as the process that builds relationships, accepts compromise, and goes beyond purely rational or logical argument.[6] Good communication and oral persuasion is like an ongoing process of inoculation, of rhetorical reinforcement. Jay Conger, a professor at the University of Southern California's Marshall School of Business, spent

12 years studying how individuals developed skills of communication and became effective leaders, team leaders, and agents of change. Focusing on language and the influence of interpersonal skills, Conger has summarized some of his key findings in the *Harvard Business Review* article, "*The Necessary Art of Persuasion.*"[7] As quoted in Conger's article, "[t]he most valuable lesson I've learned about persuasion over the years is that there's just as much strategy in how you present your position as in the position itself. In fact, I'd say the strategy of presentation is the most critical."[8] Communication requires that you gain the trust of your audience, discover what motivates them, and couch your message accordingly. As James Kouzes and Barry Posner succinctly remind us, "[l]eaders understand that unless they communicate and share information with their constituents, few will take an interest in what's going on."[9]

Former congressman Leon Panetta reaffirms the importance of knowing your audience:

> If I'm talking to a conservative from the South, who represents a rural area, and I can say, "Look, we've got something here for your farmers; but, at the same time, we have to raise revenues…in order to take care of the bigger picture that you care about. Because in the end as a conservative, you care about whether or not the deficit goes down. You care about whether we have fiscal responsibility. And, we're trying to take care of your farmers, but, more importantly, we're trying to take care of that larger issue." So you've got to find a way to appeal to that person.

> And you do the same thing on the left: if somebody cares about funding for AIDS, if they care about funding for healthcare, you've got to provide some room for that; but, at the same time, you've got to make them understand that there is also this bigger picture that they've got to focus on for the sake of the country. And the people who are successful at doing that are the ones who can then bring people together and can build that consensus that you need.

From Panetta's perspective, the process of persuasion and negotiation are also at the heart of our democracy and its values. As leaders try to reconcile their own concerns with those of the larger polity, their client, and the greater good, they are seeking to build a consensus from disparate and diverging views. People that choose sides rather than build a consensus can be good at arguing and staking out divided ground but ineffective at persuading and finding solutions. A Leading Lawyer will not rely solely on one persuasive technique, like advocacy, but will instead have the ability to employ the most appropriate persuasive technique depending on their audience and their message.

The key to an effective presentation strategy is to acknowledge your audience: judge, client, opposing party, or stakeholders. Your position, no matter how brilliant and unassailable, will not "speak for itself"; you must deliver your message to a person or a group. As a lawyer, you are usually communicating with specific people in specific circumstances, and your means of communication should take into account their expectations, needs, limitations, and biases. The more you know about and interact with your audience, the better you can organize your presentation to maximize your persuasion.

2. Communication for Everyday Use

Leadership communication often takes place day to day while you cultivate professional relationships with employees, peers, clients, and other professionals. There are a variety of skills that allow you to communicate in an informal (or less formal) environment that will open the door for future persuasion opportunities. Advocacy can sometimes be useful in these circumstances but businesslike, nonconfrontational speech is generally more effective.

In these everyday communications, it is a good idea to *focus on solving problems,*[10] not fixing people. When you need to criticize, temper it whenever possible with equal amounts of encouragement. It is human nature to respond poorly to personal criticism, but criticism of work, when mixed with positive reinforcement, tends to make people more open to feedback; they can see the criticism as an opportunity to step up rather than a dressing down. This style of supportive communication is effective because "most people are more receptive to a discussion of what can be done to change a work method, than to a discussion of what can be done to change them"[11] personally. Convey criticism in constructive, rather than destructive, ways as opportunities for improvement, rather than conclusions about someone's worth.[12]

Be specific;[13] accomplishments are best achieved in manageable steps and those steps are best completed when the audience clearly understands what is needed from them. Specify what works well or needs to be improved, rather than giving an overall evaluation, such as "your work isn't good."[14] If you specify what you expect to change, as well as ways you can help the person improve, you are much less likely to alienate and much more likely to get the results you want.

Be descriptive, not critical;[15] factual descriptions of shortcomings in work product are more easily received and improved upon than characterizations of personal deficiencies. *Be in sync;*[16] leaders have greater credibility and communicate better when their words align with their nonverbal signals. A smile and a calm demeanor will go a lot further than signs of conflict or shiftiness. *Provide validation;*[17] there are both brutal and painless ways to let someone down. It takes little effort to give words of encouragement when you chose to reject a proposal and a cutting remark may be remembered for years.

Furthermore, be *smooth and open;*[18] the interaction inherent in productive communication is disrupted and hindered when one person monopolizes the floor. Minimize interference by tempering interruptions, cross-talk, and long pauses that sidetrack people's train of thought. *Listen at least as much as you talk;*[19] it takes more effort than you might think, but it is worth the trouble. Listening gives you the gift of other people's experience and insight. That means you obtain better information and a broader perspective for dealing with the situation at hand. By listening, you will also build up a store of good will by giving others the gratification of feeling significant and the opportunity to participate.[20]

Not only are these concepts of communication useful in daily interactions with your clients, team members, and other constituents, but they are applicable at times when you seek to be more persuasive. Consider how you would use these communication skills as you read through the elements and techniques of persuasion.

3. The Elements of Persuasion

Persuasion skills are a subset of communication skills. While communication is the act of transmitting your message or the exchange of information to another person,[21] persuasion is the act of convincing another person of a belief or course of action.[22] The ability to persuade is a valuable technique for lawyers and a handy skill to have when advocacy alone is insufficient. Effective persuasion involves several distinct and essential steps that vary depending on the model in which you are operating. I have provided two basic, and highly effective, models of persuasion, constructed by Jay Conger and Robert Cialdini, each of whom are well-known social scientists in the business and academic worlds. While not all of the elements in each model will always be directly applicable in the daily life of a Leading Lawyer, I include them in order to provide you with a complete picture of these excellent and proven persuasion models.

a. JAY CONGER: The Necessary Art of Persuasion

Jay Conger's model describes persuasion as four steps. First, effective persuaders establish credibility. Second, they frame their goals in a way that identifies common ground with those they intend to persuade. Third, they connect emotionally with their audience. Fourth, they reinforce their positions using vivid language and compelling evidence.[23]

1. *Be credible.* A persuader who advocates a new or contrarian position must have high credibility. As discussed in Chapter Three, credibility requires demonstration of integrity, expertise, and dynamism. A demonstrated history of sound judgment, success, and knowledge shows that persuaders are well informed about their proposals. Cultivating solid and professional relationships also helps to build credibility. According to Conger, "people with high credibility have demonstrated, usually over time that they can be trusted to listen and to work in the best interests of others."[24] Conger notes that persuasive leaders "have also consistently shown strong emotional character and integrity...Indeed, people who are known to be honest, steady, and reliable have an edge when going into any persuasion situation. Because their relationships are robust, they are more apt to be given the benefit of the doubt."[25]

There is no formula for making up deficits in relationships but Conger says short-term steps can be taken to shore up relationships. You can meet individually with each of the key people whose support you want to win. However, do so to solicit their views, not to pitch your position. When you can, offer assistance to those you wish to persuade and ask about their concerns. Finally, you can make a special effort to involve colleagues or other counsel on your behalf who have stronger relationships with the audience and who can help deliver your message. While there is no single act that will make you more credible, saying what you mean and meaning what you say is always a good start. The combination of expertise and strong relationships based on integrity and dynamism makes a leader credible, and credibility is persuasive.

2. *Frame for common ground.* Even if your credibility is high, your position must still appeal strongly to the people you are trying to persuade.[26] Effective persuaders must be adept at describing their positions in terms that illuminate their advantages.[27] According to Conger, "[a]t the heart of framing is a solid understanding of your audience."[28] Even before starting to persuade, the best persuaders closely studied the issues that matter to their colleagues and those they are trying to persuade.[29] They use conversations, meetings, and other forms of dialogue to collect essential information.[30] They are good at listening; they test their ideas with trusted confidants and ask questions of the people they will later be persuading.[31]

By looking at the other party's perspective, you also free yourself from your own preconceptions and self-imposed obstacles. "Social psychologists have documented the difficulty most people have understanding the other side's perspective. From the trenches, successful negotiators concur that overcoming this self-centered tendency is critical."[32] This limitation afflicts lawyers all the more because our natural tendency to see our own side of things is reinforced by the need to be zealous advocates for a client and, in effect, blind ourselves to the merits of our adversary's point of view. To see past that blind-spot, and to circumvent the limitations on communication that the advocacy model tends to impose, you should "solve the other side's [problems] as the means to solving your own."[33]

Conger believes that understanding the situation and the audience is a crucial aspect of persuasion. For the message to be well-received, it should be framed as meeting one or more needs of those whose agreement is sought. As a result, their needs must be met. Leading Lawyers seek to gain an understanding of the needs of their client, their opponents, and all stakeholders in order to frame their solution in a way that satisfies many of their needs in order to be the most persuasive. This is especially true in negotiations; people settle cases for their reasons not yours. Understanding the other side's interests as well as their lawyer's legal arguments is very helpful. Responding to their issues and satisfying their needs is a crucial part of the negotiation as well as an essential element to persuasion.

3. *Provide accessible evidence.* Evidence is almost always the crux of persuasion. It is best not to present your proposals or conclusions in terms of inflexible demands or fait accompli but explain your rationales. That way, you

sell the cause instead of imposing it. People are not persuaded by conclusions, but by the explanation of how you arrived at your conclusion and why it matters.

Conger and others have also found that a cold recitation of information, however strong on the merits, typically does not make the strongest case: "[T]he most effective persuaders use language in a particular way. They supplement numerical data with examples, stories, metaphors and analogies to make their positions come alive. That use of language paints a vivid word picture and, in so doing, lends a compelling and tangible quality to the persuader's point of view."[34] Make your pitch accessible by providing not only hard data, but also a compelling story about the data. Sell your approach by highlighting its most appealing aspects, its potential, the effect it will have, and the human dimension of your strategy.

For instance William Loris, director-general of the International Development Law Organization (IDLO), was asked during a meeting with the Assistant Deputy of the State Department from whom he was seeking funding, to report on the progress that the organization had been making to help to institute the rule of law in Afghanistan. Loris described reports that had been generated, methods of assessing the quality of opinions that were being written, and his general feeling that progress was being made. However, to better illustrate his point, Loris transitioned to telling a simple, but powerful story.

> The IDLO has been in Kabul working with 30 Afghan judges. Many of them had not attended law school because they were Muslim judges in the Islamic tradition. We provided the judges with a case study to illustrate issues that would be addressed by the newly enacted criminal procedure code. The new code included all of the individual rights that you would expect in a modern legal system. The fact pattern of the case consisted of police entering a home without a warrant, discovering stolen goods, and arresting a young boy, the resident of the house, for theft. The police did not offer the boy an opportunity to speak with a lawyer, nor did they inform the boy of his charges.
>
> When the judges were asked how they would rule they all agreed and said, "Guilty. Give them the maximum penalty."

The teacher of the class, a Moroccan Muslim and member of the Supreme Court asked the judges why they would disregard the criminal procedure code and they said that "It's a waste of time, and it's a waste of public money. Just put them in jail."

In response, the teacher told a story that would illustrate his point, that following the code was necessary to the order of the criminal justice system. He used an example that spoke to the Afghan judges and persuaded each of them to reevaluate the importance of the rule of law. He said, "What if you go to the mosque, and you don't wash your feet? You don't face the right way? Instead of facing to Mecca, you face to New York? And you don't incline, bend down and touch your forehead at the right moments? ...[O]ur religion is about submission. And what if you don't do that? Will Allah retain your prayers in the same way?...The way we pray is important."

In comparing the rules of the criminal system to the rules of their sacred religion, the judges began to understand the teacher's perspective and to accept his points as valid. They were then sent back to their discussion groups and allowed more time to make a decision. After a very thoughtful discussion, the leader of the Afghan judges stood up and conceded that the comparison between the rules of the court and the rules of religion brought up an interesting point because the judges agreed that their religion would fall apart if it was not practiced with discipline. They firmly believed that the truth would be found in the criminal case in the same way and the group agreed to follow the criminal procedure code.

In making his vivid comparison between the rule of law and the rules of religion, the teacher was able to persuade the Afghan judges to completely change their attitude toward the new criminal procedure code. Also, in telling the teacher's story to the decision makers at the State Department, Loris was able to more effectively demonstrate the progress that was being made in Afghanistan than if he had delivered more data from his reports.

4. *Connect emotionally.* There is a strong emotional component to making decisions, which lawyers often overlook. We lawyers are trained to be wary of emotions, and we shortchange our understanding of human experience and our ability to persuade. Good persuaders are aware of the primacy of emotions and are responsive to them. They show their own emotional commitment to the position they are advocating.[35] Without this demonstration, people may wonder if you actually believe in the position you are championing.[36] Effective persuaders have a strong and accurate sense of their audience's emotional state, and they adjust the tone of their arguments accordingly.[37] The idea is that whatever your position, you match your emotional levels to your audience's ability to receive the message.[38] The best persuaders in Conger's study would usually canvass key individuals who had a good pulse on the mood and emotional expectations of those about to be persuaded.[39] They would ask those individuals how various proposals might affect their audience on an emotional basis—in essence, testing possible reactions.[40] They were also quite effective at gathering information through informal conversations.[41] In the end, their aim was to ensure that the emotional appeal behind their persuasion matched what their audience was already feeling or expecting.[42] For high-impact persuasion and communication, textbook author DuBrin provides one last piece of advice.

DuBrin's recommendation is to use a ladder of techniques.[43] Research shows that in many cases, persuasion approaches should be used in succession as necessary: 1) introduce the subject with reason; 2) be logical; 3) use moderate force; and 4) strike a bargain. This sequence ensures that escalation occurs only as required and the dialogue never gets out of hand. Escalate to more high-pressure or argumentative strategies *only* once you have exhausted the more low-key, persuasive ones. "Begin with the most positive, or least abrasive, tactic. If you do not gain the advantage you seek, proceed to a stronger tactic...."[44] Keep in mind that abrasive tactics trigger revenge and retaliation[45] and should be avoided if possible. Consequently, start with a rational appeal, move to emotional empathic arguments, and later use even more aggressive techniques if necessary. It is not recommended that you start out with threats and oppressive techniques.

Persuasion is a more effective form of communication than coercion. Using coercive techniques on employees, coworkers, or even opposing lawyers and their clients will likely result in backlash or resentment. Persuasion allows people to voluntarily, perhaps stubbornly, agree to your ideas. Leading Lawyers understand their preferred style of communication but are able to adjust in order to best persuade their audience and effect positive change. In litigation, it is best to start out rationally and then move to the more assertive and confrontational modes, if necessary. In order to have the most impact on their audience, a Leading Lawyer must recognize which method of communication and persuasion to employ, when to switch gears, and how to convince the listener while presenting such information in a credible and verbally appealing way. Leading Lawyers seek to master these subtle skills of persuasive communication in order to effect positive change for their clients, organization, and community.

b. ROBERT CIALDINI: Influence

Another well-known and utilized model of persuasion was developed by Robert Cialdini. Under the Cialdini method of persuasion, there are six basic tendencies of human behavior that come into play in generating a positive and persuaded response: 1) reciprocation, 2) consistency, 3) social validation, 4) liking, 5) authority, and 6) scarcity.[46] As these six tendencies help to govern our business dealings, our social involvements, and our personal relationships, knowledge of the rules of persuasion can be truly effective.

1. *Reciprocation*: All societies subscribe to a norm that obligates individuals to repay in kind what they have received. Each of us has been taught to live up to the rule, and each of us knows the social sanctions and derision applied to anyone who violates it.[47] Because there is a general distaste for those who take, and make no effort to give in return, we will often go to great lengths to avoid being considered a moocher, ingrate, or freeloader.[48] At the top, elected officials engage in "logrolling" and an exchange of favors that makes politics the place of strange bedfellows indeed.[49] The out-of-character vote of one of our elected representatives on a bill or measure can often be understood as a favor returned to the bill's sponsor.[50] Cialdini provided a perfect example of the human tendency to reciprocate favors:

> *Political analysts were amazed at Lyndon Johnson's success in getting to many of his programs through Congress during his early administration. Even members of Congress who were thought to be strongly opposed to the proposals*

*were voting for them. Close examination by political scien-
tists has found the cause to be not so much Johnson's political
savvy as the large score of favors he had been able to provide
to other legislators during his many years of power in the
House and Senate.*[51]

Another form of reciprocation that Cialdini highlights does not involve the
exchange of gifts or favors, but an exchange of concessions. He used a personal
story to illustrate:

*I was walking down the street when I was approached by
a...boy...selling tickets to the annual Boy Scouts Circus...He
asked if I wished to buy any tickets at $5 apiece. Since one of
the last places I wanted to spend a Saturday evening was with
the Boy Scouts, I declined. "Well," he said, if you don't want
to buy any tickets, how about buying some of our chocolate
bars? They're only $1 each." I bought a couple and, right
away, realized that something noteworthy had happened. I
knew that to be the case because (a) I do not like chocolate
bars; (b) I do like dollars; (c) I was standing there with two
of his chocolate bars; and (d) he was walking away with two
of my dollars.*[52]

As Cialdini found out from his interaction with the boy scout, another
consequence of the rule of reciprocity is an obligation to make a concession to
someone who has made a concession to us.[53] A Leading Lawyer might employ
these techniques of reciprocity with minimal effort and in a variety of ways,
such as helping a colleague with an issue or conceding a small point to an opposing party. Anything the lawyer chooses to do for someone else will open the
door to future reciprocation and persuasion opportunities.

2. *Consistency*: Public commitments, even seemingly minor ones, direct
future action.[54] Whenever one takes a stand that is visible to others, there arises
a drive to maintain that stand in order to *look* like a consistent person. Within
the realm of compliance, securing an initial commitment is the key.[55] After
making a commitment, people are more willing to agree to requests that are
in keeping with the prior commitment.[56] Thus, many compliance professionals
try to induce people to take an initial position that is consistent with a behavior

they will later request from these people.[57] Not all commitments are equally effective, however, in producing consistent future action.[58] Commitments are most effective when they are active, public, effortful, and viewed as internally motivated (uncoerced).[59]

In this sense, a Leading Lawyer will refrain from committing himself until he is confident that he will follow through with the commitment. He also recognizes that gaining a commitment from an opponent or other stakeholder early in the negotiation or issue resolution will provide leverage if the stakeholder begins to act inconsistently.

3. *Social validation*: One fundamental way that we decide what to do in a situation is to look to what others are doing or have done before.[60] If many individuals have decided in favor of a particular idea, we are more likely to follow because we perceive the idea to be more correct, more valid.[61] Cialdini points out that, as a rule, we make fewer mistakes by acting in accord with social evidence than by acting contrary to it.[62] If you can show that your position is consistent with industry standards or has been successful in similar or plausibly related situations, the proposed change will be more persuasive. A Leading Lawyer will highlight the similarity of their facts to legal precedence or custom during persuasion opportunities.

4. *Liking*: People prefer to say yes to those they like.[63] In a related corollary, making the opposite side upset or angry, for no good reason, is not helpful to persuasion. Those who wish to commission the power of liking employ tactics clustered about certain factors that research has shown to work.[64] Similarity, compliments, and cooperation are factors that have been shown to enhance positive feelings and behavior.[65] According to Cialdini, a Leading Lawyer who looks credible and polished will gain a persuasive edge. Also, highlight the similarities between yourself and your views with those of whom you seek to persuade. Being cooperative with your audience and providing compliments when warranted and genuine also contributes to liking and is persuasive.

This idea was also presented by Andrew DuBrin in his text *Leadership*. Without misrepresenting or fawning, convey your appreciation for what you find commendable in their efforts. For example, Vickie Patton, an attorney working for the Environmental Defense Fund with Fred Krupp, was working diligently to push through a piece of legislation called the Clear Air Interstate Rule. The legislation was designed to reduce the sulfur and nitrogen pollution in the United State's eastern 29 states by 70%. President George W. Bush's administration helped to enact the legislation under authority provided by the

Clean Air Act. Despite a trend of falling on opposite sides of environmental issues, Krupp (under Patton's advice) acknowledged in a press conference that the Bush administration had been instrumental in implementing the much needed interstate rule. This deserved praise kept the door open for the EDF and the Bush administration to work collaboratively in the future.

5. *Expertise and authority*: Those touting their experience, expertise, or scientific credentials are trying to harness the power of authority. There is nothing wrong with such claims when they are real because people usually want the opinions of true authorities.[66] Their insights help us choose quickly and well.[67] It is frequently adaptive to obey the dictates of genuine authorities because such individuals usually possess high levels of knowledge, wisdom, and power.[68] We have seen how expertise is useful to bolster credibility in Chapter Three, and now both Conger and Cialdini have demonstrated how expertise can also be persuasive. A Leading Lawyer who is an expert in their field can use that knowledge to their persuasive advantage.

6. *Scarcity*: A great deal of evidence shows that items and opportunities become more desirable to us as they become less available.[69] For this reason, marketers trumpet the unique benefits or the one-of-a-kind character of their offerings.[70] Almost everyone is vulnerable to the scarcity principle in some form. Take as evidence the experience of Florida State University students who, like most undergraduates when surveyed, rated the quality of their campus cafeteria food unsatisfactory. Nine days later, according to a second survey, they had changed their minds.[71] Something had happened to make them like their cafeteria's food significantly better than before.[72] Interestingly, the event that caused them to shift their opinions had nothing to do with the quality of the food service, which had not changed,[73] but its availability had. On the day of the second survey, the students had learned that, because of a fire, they could not eat at the cafeteria for the next two weeks making it far scarcer.[74] In the world of real estate, we see claims of one-of-a-kind houses and rare finds. In the legal field, we often declare "last chance" for a settlement before trial or expensive discovery processes or put a timeline on an offer, in an effort to make the deal scarce.

4. Conclusion

Most lawyers believe that advocacy is the best way to communicate their ideas because that is what they were taught in law school and it is what they most commonly see in practice. However, Leading Lawyers know that communication is more than advocacy; there is a time for sticking to your guns and advocating hard for your position and a time for alternative persuasion techniques. How one presents their message should depend on a multitude of factors including the environment in which the message is being given, the audience to which it is being delivered, and the subject matter that is being presented.

Leading Lawyers recognize that communication is strategic and persuasive. Knowing the various ways in which people interact, being cognizant of our own communication style and the effect it has each day, and designing your proposal to have a persuasive impact on each audience member, are skills integral to a Leading Lawyer's success.

Notes

[1.] See Gary Yukl and J. Bruce Tracey, "Consequences of Influence Tactics Used With Subordinates, Peers and the Boss", *Journal of Applied Psychology*, 525-535 (August, 1992); *see also* Andrew J. DuBrin, *Leadership*, 249 Houghlin and Mifflin (4th ed. 2004).

[2.] DuBrin, *supra* note 1 at 249.

[3.] Robert B. Cialdini, "Harnessing the Science of Persuasion", *Harvard Business Review*, 77 (October 2001).

[4.] *Id.* at 79.

[5.] *Id.*

[6.] Jay Conger, "The Necessary Art of Persuasion", *Harvard Business Review*, 87 (May-June 1988).

[7.] *Id.*

[8.] *Id.* at 87-88.

[9.] James Kouzes and Barry Posner, *Credibility: How Leaders Gain and Lose it, Why People Demand It*, 172 Jossey-Bass (2003).

[10.] DuBrin, *supra* note 1 at 367-77.

[11.] *Id.* at 375.

[12.] *Id.* at 376.

[13.] *Id.* at 367-77.

[14.] *Id.* at 377.

[15.] *Id.* at 367-77.

[16.] *Id.*

17. *Id.*

18. *Id.*

19. *Id.*

20. *Id.*

21. Merriam-Webster Online, *available at* http://www.merriam-webster.com/dictionary/communication (accessed September 2008).

22. Merriam-Webster Online, *available at* http://www.merriam-webster.com/dictionary/persuasion (accessed September 2008).

23. Conger, *supra* note 7 at 87-90.

24. *Id.*

25. *Id.* at 88.

26. *Id.* at 90.

27. *Id.*

28. *Id.*

29. *Id.* at 91.

30. *Id.*

31. *Id.* at 91-92.

32. James K. Sebenius, "Six Habits of Merely Effective Negotiators", *Harvard Business Review*, 88 (April 2001).

33. *Id.* at 89.

34. Conger, *supra* note 7 at 92.

35. *Id.* at 93.

36. *Id.*

37. *Id.*

38. *Id.*

39. *Id.*

40. *Id.*

41. *Id.*

42. *Id.*

43. DuBrin, *supra* note 1 at 249-250.

44. *Id.* at 250.

45. *Id.*

46. Robert Cialdini, *Influence*, Allyn & Bacon (4th ed. 2001).

47. *Id.* at 21-22.

48. *Id.*

49. *Id.* at 26.

50. *Id.*

51. *Id.*

52. *Id.* at 36-37.

53. *Id.* at 37.

54. Robert Cialdini, "The Science Persuasion", *Scientific American Mind*, 32-39 (January 2004), *also available at* http://www.sciam.com.

55. Cialdini, *supra* note 46 at 37.

56. *Id.*

57. *Id.*

58. *Id.*

59. *Id.*

60. Cialdini, *supra* note 54.

61. *Id.*

62. Cialdini, *supra* note 46 at 37.

63. Cialdini, *supra* note 54.

64. *Id.*

65. *Id.*

66. *Id.*

67. *Id.*

68. Cialdini, *supra* note 46 at 201.

69. Cialdini, *supra* note 54.

70. *Id.*

71. Cialdini, *supra* note 46 at 204.

72. *Id.*

73. *Id.*

74. *Id.*

CHAPTER SEVEN:
Collaborate with and Motivate Others Through Relationships and Team Building

Relationship-building, team-building, collaboration, motivation, and emotional awareness are all important aspects of a Leading Lawyer's ability to be successful in implementing solutions and creating change. We may not have thought we needed these skills when we decided to go to law school, and many of us continue to scoff at assertions that team- and relationship-building are essential for success, but the need for these skills has been thrust upon us by our clients, and those of us who excel in these areas will accomplish more than those of us who do not. The success of a deal, the litigation of a conflict, the merger of companies, and the overall health of any organization (including your law organization) is intimately intertwined with improving teams, understanding people, managing and building positive relationships, and shaping the culture of an organization. The most effective skills used in producing results require human interaction. Leading Lawyers understand that in today's world, successful lawyers are not only expert technical practitioners but they are also relationship builders and team builders who interact positively with and motivate others.

In his book, *Know How*, Ram Charan[1] acknowledges the necessity of interpersonal

"One of the main things we do is maintain our relationships because we have an enormous amount of them. At the International Development Law Organization we have 17,000 alumni; they are established into foundations in 42 countries. We keep in touch with them and encourage them to take the lead."

William Loris
Director-General of the International Development Law Organization

"The Environmental Defense Fund is often out to solve the problems of endangered species and ...you might not expect us to work with land owners or business or community groups...but when you think about it, they are clearly the most important people for us to work with."

Fred Krupp
President of the Environmental Defense Fund

111

skills when he lists "eight skills that separate people who perform from people who don't."[2] Charan's insight into the real content of leadership outlines eight fundamental skills needed for commercial success in the 21st century. Those skills are: *Positioning* (and when necessary, repositioning) your business by zeroing in on the central idea that meets customer needs and makes money; *pinpointing patterns of external change* ahead of others; *leading the social system and culture* of your business by shaping the way people work together; *judging people* by getting to the truth of a person; *creating a working team of leaders* by molding high-energy, high-powered, high-ego people to equal more than the sum of their parts; *developing goals* that balance what the business can become with what it can realistically achieve; *setting laser-sharp priorities* that become the road map for meeting your goals; and *dealing creatively and positively with societal pressures* that go beyond the economic value-creation activities of your business. It is important to notice that four of Charan's eight essential skill sets are **people- and society-driven.**

Furthermore, consider the research by Robert Kelley of Bell Labs. Kelley's research looked at the productivity of scientists, all experts in their field, and found that the engineers who were most successful (dubbed "stars") were not those with the highest IQs. The "stars" developed strong networks within the organization and worked with others in a totally different manner from the more average performers. Some of the interpersonal skills demonstrated by the "stars" included: helping colleagues solve a problem or complete a task; giving others credit for their success; expressing a desire to hear others' ideas; listening and not imposing their ideas on others; utilizing the skills of coworkers; and putting the objectives of the team before their own. Leading Lawyers understand, just as the "stars" at Bell Labs did, that they do not operate in a vacuum; they build relationships, take the initiative, collaborate, and motivate others to act.[3]

Leading Lawyers have mastered these concepts and find success in their abilities to:

1) **Build Relationships.** It is difficult for busy lawyers to take the time to develop relationships. Yet this is an effective step to successful leadership. Leading Lawyers make time to develop relationships in every setting. They also develop relationships before they need them. With a network of relationships and a history of working cooperatively to

help others with their own projects and programs, Leading Lawyers receive the support they need to make their projects successful.

2) **Collaborate and Compromise with Opposing Counsel and Their Clients.** Leading Lawyers work hard to build relationships and their first approach in any situation is collaborative; even in situations of conflict. This is the model used by most business clients and has certainly become the industry standard in business negotiations and other areas of business interaction. Leading Lawyers seek to listen and understand the needs of the other side. They also create partnerships where they previously did not exist and seek new solutions and opportunities for all stakeholders.

3) **Rely upon and Motivate Their Team and Organization.** Virtually every major project and important change involves engaging, persuading, and working with other people. Leading Lawyers create enthusiasm for the work at hand. They help clients and team members see challenges in a positive light and develop opportunities for achievement and transformation. They encourage all employees to create opportunity and lead the client or company to newfound success. High-achieving organizations are motivated to embrace change, and Leading Lawyers know how to inspire their organization toward long-term success.

4) **Effectively Use Emotional IQ.** Research has shown that being the most intelligent person does not guarantee success in the future. Another important predictor of success is a person's ability to control and manage their own emotions and relate to others. This ability has been dubbed "emotional IQ." Letting one's emotions rule and get out of control can defeat the most intelligent lawyer.

1. Building Relationships

Leading lawyers have an ability to build large networks from both their social and professional interactions. These networks include lawyers from their own firm and others, current and past clients, people from a variety of industries, judges, law school and personal friends, professional associations and organizations, and even family members. Leading Lawyers rely upon their network of relationships and they make an effort to create and exchange value in each relationship. Trying to build a connection with the sole purpose of gaining a competitive advantage is misguided and will not result in a fruitful relationship. These types of interactions are impersonal, short-term, and self-involved.[4] The goal is to build a relationship without the expectation of immediate benefits. A Leading Lawyer knows that effective networking is about building long-term, personal, and mutually beneficial relationships with the people with whom they interact frequently.

There are some basic tenets to building a network based on meaningful relationships. The first tenet is **authenticity**: people are drawn to those that are sincere and genuine[5] and can detect insincerity and ulterior motives. The second is that networking **trades in resources.**[6] A network prospers when there is reciprocity among the members. Providing recommendations or referrals for other lawyers based on their particular skill set will set the tone for reciprocity. Third, networking requires **creating deliberate and personal opportunities for networking**. Relying on networking Web sites or alumni directories as a guide for how well you are connecting with people will lead to false assurances.[7] The number of contacts you have means little if you do not have an actual relationship with them. Fourth, networking requires skillful **communication**.[8] Effective communication is a two-way street: a lawyer should posses the abilities of an excellent speaker but also a respectful listener. The relationships with members of a network would be weakened if the communication channels only worked in one direction. Lastly, networking calls for **negotiating skill**.[9] Knowing when to perform favors and when to hold back keeps the relationship from becoming one-sided.

It is important to understand that there are some natural barriers to building effective relationships within a network. The adversarial nature of law often creates a competitive atmosphere which can hinder the development of relationships and a broad network. We have to sometimes fight our competitive tendencies and show courtesy and respect for the other parties involved so that even litigation will lend itself to creating meaningful relationships. The person across the courtroom may someday be a co-counsel or on the other side of a collaborative deal and it is best to avoid burning bridges by first adopting a warlike demeanor. Building a relationship with every partner and associate in a firm or other network may not be feasible. Focus on those with whom you can find common ground and practice synergy. Furthermore, it may be difficult to bring some opposing counsel or other colleagues into your network if they do not share the same enlightened views of mutual respect. Building relationships should not involve strategy, tedious activities, or a façade; they should be genuinely developed with patience, intent, and through personal contact.

In an article titled, "The Transatlantic Elite,"[10] published by Lawyer.com, extensive research was done to identify the 16 most successful trans-Atlantic law firms in the United States and Europe. Alan Klein of Simpson Thacher & Bartlet (one of the 16) noted in the piece that the success of the elite firms highlights the importance of building relationships. Frequently, there are the same faces involved in the major trans-Atlantic M&A deals and it is important to maintain positive relationships with all stakeholders, including opposing counsel. For example, Klein told the story of how he was once hired on a very large M&A deal, not because he represented either of the two corporations but because he held a long-term relationship with the underwriting bankers. "'We were hired the same day,' recalls Klein. 'Why? Their bankers, UBS, knew us.'" This is a perfect illustration of why it is a good idea to build relationships with everyone involved in a deal. A Leading Lawyer recognizes how investing in a network of cordial working-relationships that require minimal effort, such as treating everyone with dignity and respect or providing a piece of advice or solution to a problem, can later produce sizeable returns.

Larry Sonsini remembers his first meeting with his clients Larry Page and Sergey Brin, who wanted to start a company they were calling Google. As Sonsini recalls their first encounters, Page and Brin came into the meeting narrowly focused on the fundamentals that they needed to accomplish. As a Leading Lawyer, Sonsini emphasizes, it is crucial to provide not only legal support, but also to help develop the right relationships and expertise in order to help the company take root and grow. Drawing on his existing network, Larry Sonsini was able to involve experienced venture capitalists, not just because they would provide financial backing but because they would bring an invaluable passion, expertise, and business judgment to the table as well. Sonsini tapped his relationships with John Doerr of Kleiner Perkins and Mike Moritz of Sequoia Capital who could deliver not only money, but advice and strategy. The relationships and contacts continued to bear fruit:

> When it came time to go public, and expand the board of directors, we talked about what kind of board Google should have. After a lot of thought, the team attracted some outstanding directors, people like Art Levinson of Genentech,

and Paul Otellini, the CEO of Intel. This is an example of a team sitting down together, bringing individual experience and expertise, and talking through the next step. Each member can provide some contacts and suggest people who can bring something to the party. So it is important to be a channel and a source.[11]

In order to facilitate the launch of one of the most successful companies the world has ever known, using his existing network of relationship, Sonsini helped to build a team whose value and expertise were diverse and far-reaching.

2. Collaborate with the "Other" Side

David Gergin, director of the Center for Leadership at Harvard, once said, "The most effective leaders are those who can cross boundaries, forming partnerships not just in their own sectors but with other sectors…as well…today's leader is usually the one sitting at a table with six others, sleeves rolled up, trying to solve a problem together."[12] Negotiations in the business world are frequently collaborative because business negotiators have taken advantage of the benefits of problem-solving over competitive negotiation.[13] There are many areas in which lawyers have the flexibility to act collaboratively. Leading Lawyers have followed their clients' push toward business collaboration. Even civil litigation can move toward more collaboration to improve the process and reduce costs.

Leading Lawyer Leon Panetta has come to a similar conclusion, emphasizing the need to go beyond the limited advocacy model in a variety of arenas. He notes that:

More and more, it's about the fight and the conflict, as opposed to whether you can play a role in resolving differences. You've got to turn to people who are willing to play that more creative role. It always appeared to me that the role of lawyers and the judge is to determine how to resolve conflict. It's not so much who wins, who loses, it's how you resolve that issue in a way that the parties can walk away, and say, "Well, the right thing happened."

It doesn't mean you shouldn't advocate on behalf of your client; it means that, in the end, the interests of justice are best served. You cannot simply take your client and go off a cliff with continued conflict. Take the interests of your client, and see if there's a way ultimately to satisfy them along with the other sides'.[14]

For Panetta, one of our key tasks as attorneys is to recognize all sides of an issue—to find ways we can be advocates for our clients, but also to help them recognize the bigger picture:

You are fighting on behalf of your particular client, but I believe that a fundamental role of our judicial system is to provide a forum in which those issues can be debated, but ultimately a forum that resolves those issues. And sometimes, one side "wins" and one side "loses," but you can ultimately look at the situation to compromise, and say, "You know, in fairness, this is what ought to happen."

And that's a role that lawyers ought to play. I don't think it's all about going to war. It shouldn't focus on perpetuating conflict. It's not about trench warfare. Ultimately, we seek the resolution of issues.[15]

Leon Panetta agrees; Leading Lawyers seek the best possible outcome for their client but also to effect positive change for all of those involved as well.

Fred Krupp, a Leading Lawyer and president of the Environmental Defense Fund, practices this principle on a near-daily basis. In a recent article in *U.S. News and World Report,* Krupp tells the story of how some of his staffers wanted to sue McDonald's over its environmentally toxic use of polystyrene sandwich boxes. Instead, Krupp chose to meet with McDonald's President Ed Resni. He chose this path with the understanding that, "[i]f we are trying to change opinions, we better understand what they think first." Eventually, the two organizations teamed up to find a solution. Krupp recalls that, in the end they did not file a report against McDonald's but *with* them. Because of Krupp's willingness to collaborate with his opponents, McDonald's has replaced its iconic clamshell package with recycled paper and, based on recommendations in the report, slashed other solid waste as well.[16]

Every person interviewed for this book advocated collaboration first, competition second, even in the most highly litigious practices. Each recognized that, as a lawyer, it is easy to fall into roles that we believe demand "winning" over doing what is right. An all too common scenario, as Panetta describes, is this: "You've got two parties that are basically locked in trench warfare. They're fighting each other. They're throwing grenades at each other. They're trying to blow each other up, and what's missing is why they're there in the first place, which isn't to just kick the hell out of each other."[17] It's to resolve issues, find common ground, to govern, and to create positive change whenever possible.

3. Team Building and Collaboration

Henry Ford said, "Coming together is a beginning. Keeping together is progress. Working together is success," and in three simple sentences, Ford defined the team-building process. A team is necessarily comprised of a group of people who associate themselves in work or activity, but people can work together and never rise to the definition of a team.[18] According to a study done by the Center for Creative Leadership, more than 97% of people in the study believed collaboration is essential to success. However, only 30% of the total respondents and 47% of senior leaders believed leaders in their organization are actually skilled in collaboration.[19] Because the ability to collaborate in a team effort is so clearly important, it is helpful to understand the key components needed to transform a group of people into a team and foster collaboration among everyone. Before collaboration can occur, a leader must build a team, create a climate of trust, and facilitate relationships.[20]

When lawyers prepare for litigation, negotiation, a business deal, or even an in-house project, they become a group, but may fail to achieve a team-building mindset. Paralegals, administrative assistants, and other support staff assist in project coordination, research, and document production. Associates assist in the "lawyering" while partners oversee the process. Further insights can come from experts, the client, or other firms that are involved. As with any team, communication, trust, and understanding between these individuals are needed for a successful solution to the identified "problem" or the accomplishment of a goal that they are collectively working toward. Without a team mindset, work will become time-consuming, stressful, redundant, and possibly even counterproductive. Leading Lawyers understand the importance of a coalition of people working together and will build a team with that goal in mind.

A fantastic example of a successful team can be found through examination of the success of the Antitrust Modernization Committee (AMC) lead by Deborah Garza of the Justice Department. Ms. Garza was hand-selected by President George W. Bush to chair the AMC, a bipartisan commission tasked to produce recommendations and a report and for the improvement of antitrust laws in the United States for Congress and the President. Her utilization of the skills necessary to bring about positive change through an effective team-building process was impeccable.

From the committee's inception, Garza's first step was to clearly communicate her vision to build a bridge between the political ideological differences and to produce a *consensus report*. She broached this subject with the commission in their first meeting together and found that all of the members were interested in producing a report that was well-received and, at the end of the day, would have an effect. They agreed that a consensus report would be the most effective.

Her second step was to produce an atmosphere of trust and collaboration within the team. When asked about the committee's members, Garza described them as "highly-respected members in the anti-trust and legal community with substantial achievements of their own who were all willing to roll up their sleeves and get involved." Garza felt that if the committee members were willing to commit time and effort to the project, then as their leader, she was determined to show her appreciation for their contribution and to ensure that their efforts were not fruitless. Garza facilitated an attitude of collaboration within the commission in which the team members listened to each other, participated openly in a dialogue, and actually ended up making recommendations that were different from their original positions. While each of them were extraordinary advocates, as demonstrated during the committee's hearings, the members refrained from being antagonistic toward each other because it was clearly established early in the process that they were "all pulling the same plow."[21]

Furthermore, Garza recognized each member's desire to get involved in various ways and she reached out to those members and brought them into the process. Garza identified how each commissioner preferred to work and what contributions would make them most comfortable and tried to orient the process to draw upon those strengths and proclivities. There were even times when Garza would purposely step back and use the teams' collective strengths to move the ball forward on an issue. She would give the commissioners the opportunity to really make progress by unleashing them, and giving them the ability to do what they needed to do for the team. As Garza put it: "So a lot of it was…not managing talent, but *enabling* them to accomplish what they needed to do but still doing it within the team."[22]

Justice Kennard also uses an extensive team process in drafting her California Supreme Court Decisions. Once an initial draft is in place it is distributed to everyone and an open brainstorming meeting takes place. This includes her chief of staff, her research attorneys, and even her interns. Long discussion and analysis take place during these meetings and the group works together to flush out the final opinion as it goes though extensive review and redrafting.[23]

In order to effectively replicate the process of creating and operating a successful team like the AMC or Justice Kennard's staff, it is helpful to understand: a) how to build a team, b) what the characteristics of a successful team are, c) how to build a trust within the group that is necessary to optimize the team's accomplishments, d) how to facilitate relationships between team members, and e) how to recognize when team members have become dysfunctional.

a. A Team-Building Model[24]

One of the first team-building models, still used today, was developed by Bruce Tuckman back in 1965. In his article, *Developmental Sequences in Small Groups*,[25] he explained the four stages a team will predictably enter in their struggle to grow, face challenges, tackle problems, find solutions, plan work, and deliver results. Tuckman explained that as a team matures and gains ability, relationships are established among the members. The team leader will alter their leadership style to operate within the current stage of the team. The terms coined by Tuckman to describe these stages are: Forming, Storming, Norming, and Performing.

Forming: This is the initial stage where the team meets and comes together. At this point, team members are highly dependent on the team leader for guidance and direction because each person's roles and responsibilities are unclear. The leader directs the process of forming the team and focuses on task orientation. The members acquaint themselves with one another and begin to form relationships. Under the direction of the team leader, the team meets to learn about the challenges and opportunities and to agree on goals. At this stage, the individual team members will behave independently.

Storming: This phase of team-building is characterized by intergroup discussions as well as some conflict. A team can pass through this stage quickly or can become bogged down indefinitely by allowing destructive behaviors to rule. At this point, the team must address what problems to solve, how to function independently and as a group, and what leadership model to adopt. Team members will volunteer different ideas to address these issues and try to establish their role and status within the group. The storming process can get stuck in power struggles, the formation of cliques or factions within the group, and focusing on minute details instead of the big picture. Individual members must be tolerant and patient of others and the team must focus on its goals to avoid becoming consumed by emotional and relationship issues. The team leader must navigate the team toward their ultimate purpose, support them during this stage, and coach them to avoid conflict and keep the process moving.

Norming: During this phase, the team members adjust their behavior, develop work habits that make teamwork cohesive, and settle into a working style. The roles and responsibilities of the individuals have clarity and major decisions are made by group agreement. Members begin to trust one another and motivation increases as people become acquainted. A loss of creativity is a potential problem during this phase if normalization of the group becomes too difficult. The leader enables the team's success by setting goals and motivating the group.

Performing: At this stage, the team can function as a unit and employs a methodology to achieve their goal smoothly and effectively without inappropriate conflict or the need for external supervision. Members are competent, interdependent, and yet autonomous. Decision-making and disagreements can be handled without supervision. As a result, the leader delegates, oversees, and challenges the team to continue improving instead of micromanaging.

As we saw above, Ms. Garza worked through each of these phases with great success. She first spent time working with each committee member, outlining the goals and vision of the committee: to develop and create a consensus report. She helped the committee to storm their way to success by allowing each of them to articulate their ideological differences and yet also be understood in their views of the direction of antitrust law in the United States. They reached their norming and performing stage after a level of trust had been established and they all worked hard, seeking to create and develop a consensus report that would be effective and well received.

Successful implementation of this team-building model is an ongoing process. Long-standing teams will go through these cycles multiple times as new circumstances for leadership arises. For lawyers, the situation may change when one case ends and another begins or when a team member leaves or new team members arrive. Furthermore, having a great team-building model does not necessarily guarantee success but it does increase its likelihood.

Beyond the traditional stages of team-building, the most effective teams tend to exhibit a pattern of recurring characteristics.

b. Eight Characteristics of an Effective Team[26]

In order to more effectively implement the team-building model, it is important to be aware of the traits and characteristics that are common among the most cohesive and accomplished teams. The Center for Creative Leadership has performed studies that consistently show eight characteristics that separate successful teams from the less successful. Those characteristics include:

1) **A Clear Mission:** the team knows what they are trying to achieve.

2) **High Performance Standards:** individual team members know how well they need to perform in order to achieve the team's mission.

3) **Resource Evaluation:** the team understands what equipment, training facilities, opportunities, and outside resources are available to help the team.

4) **Assessment of the Technical Skills of Team Members:** leaders determine what technical skills each team member possesses.

5) **Securing Resources and Equipment:** the team secures resources and equipment necessary for team effectiveness.

6) **Planning and Organizing:** a plan is devised to make optimal use of available resources, to select new members with needed technical skills, or to improve needed technical skills of existing members.

7) **High Levels of Communication:** leaders help team members stay focused on the mission and take better advantage of the skills, knowledge, and resources available to the team.

8) **Minimization of Interpersonal Conflicts in the Team:** high levels of communication and resolution helps to avoid conflict that drains energy needed for team success and effectiveness.

The first six characteristics are primarily concerned with task accomplishment. The last two are concerned with group maintenance or interpersonal aspects of the team. Effective teams that exhibit these eight positive characteristics are also successful when there is a climate of trust developed in the group.

c. Create a Climate of Trust

A leader cannot lead if no one is willing to follow or take their direction. In order for people to feel comfortable enough to make a commitment to a leader, trust must first be established. When a leader builds a climate of trust, team members will feel free to be innovative and will contribute more to the team.

There are several ways in which you can work toward building a climate of trust among team members. For instance, *be the first to trust*. Being the first to trust is difficult because it requires you to be vulnerable and release some control. A leader must set an example by stating what they believe, admitting to mistakes, asking for both positive and negative feedback, sharing information, and acknowledging the contributions of others.[27] Next, *establish a learning environment*. Establishing an environment where it is acceptable to ask questions and make mistakes is conducive to a trusting environment. When people are fearful of repercussions for mistakes, their focus is not on learning from such errors, but preventing their discovery. Also, *be open to influence*. A leader should be open to influence and willing to consider alternate viewpoints. By being open to influence themselves and utilizing others' expertise and abilities, a leader builds trust that will be reciprocated by team members' increased willingness to be influenced.[28] Finally, *share resources*. Establish early on that sharing information and resources is to everyone's benefit. Leaders should not see themselves as the sole source of information for their team. Share the means of obtaining the relevant information.

A leader must remember that in order to foster an environment of trust, they must themselves be trusting, listen to their team members, provide them with the necessary training and support, and then step back and let them be responsible for their own jobs.

d. Facilitate Relationships

A leader must also establish a sense of interdependence within the team. Impart members with the understanding that they cannot singularly succeed without the group succeeding as a whole. Lily Cheng of PACE Learning & Consultancy put it best when she said, "To be successful, teams must adopt a 'we will win' mind-set, and not an 'I, me, myself' mind-set."[29] To create interdependence, a leader must develop cooperative goals and roles, support norms of reciprocity, structure projects to promote joint efforts, and support face-to-face interactions.[30] To develop cooperative goals and roles, focus on a collective purpose that binds people to cooperative efforts.[31] A leader must instill the idea that each individual and their contributions is a unique and necessary piece of the group puzzle. As pointed out by Robert Grey:

> If you're going to lead an effort that is going to have a dramatic impact on an entire system, you have to think about who it is that's going to be affected. And, you have to reach out and convince them that their being a part of it is not only important, but critical to its success.[32]

Reciprocity requires an equal give-and-take among all team members. The relationship breaks down if one person is always giving, and another always taking. When one person helps another to succeed, acknowledges their accomplishments, and helps them shine in front of others, the norm of reciprocity is established. Because people are more likely to cooperate when the benefits of working together outweigh the benefits of working alone,[33] a leader should *promote joint efforts* but structure projects so that each person's contributions are visible in the end result; acknowledge individual efforts, but ultimately reward the end product. Emphasizing the long-term benefits will foster a cooperative mindset for all team members.[34] Lastly, *engage in face-to-face interactions* because, "[u]ntil you see someone's face, they are not a real person to you."[35] A trusting relationship is best established in person. There exists a greater sense of responsibility between two people who have met versus people who have only interacted over the phone or email. Leaders should encourage members to work together and talk in person instead of shielding themselves with e-mail. Effective teams that exhibit all the positive characteristics can, however, be hindered if the team is not purged of four dysfunctional roles that team members sometimes develop.

e. Dysfunctional Roles

Leading Lawyers realize that good delegation requires team members to take a leadership role. Effective leaders will refrain from interfering with a team process but they will not allow a dysfunctional team member's behavior that serves selfish or egocentric, rather than group, purposes[36] to destroy the effectiveness of the group.

There are four main types of inefficient conduct that a team member can engage in. The first occurs when a member *monopolizes group time* or forces their views on others. Another involves a member stubbornly *obstructing or impeding group work* or engaging in persistent negativism. A member who belittles others and/or *creates a hostile or intimidating work environment* is another example of a dysfunctional role. Lastly, a member who engages in *irrelevant or distracting behaviors* also hinders productivity. These behaviors can throw a wrench in each stage of the team-building model and prevent a team from successfully moving forward. It is often a mistake on the team leader's part to ignore these dysfunctional members or assume that the team can move forward despite their behavior. A leader must be willing to discipline or remove the poisonous member so that they do not bring the entire team to a frustrating halt.

Dysfunctional behavior is sometimes the earmark of litigation but it need not be. One of my experiences with dysfunctional team behavior took place in a negotiation when I was a young lawyer. An attorney from New Orleans named Richard Dicharry represented Lloyds of London in a case involving a very large toxic spill in Northern California. The case had been going on for several months and the group of defense attorneys, of which I was a member, had developed a good working relationship with the plaintiff's and became involved in a positive problem-solving approach. Richard, along with others, had provided positive leadership and I took note of his tactics. Not only was he an excellent lawyer but he exemplified the traits of a Leading Lawyer.

About midway through the case, a new lawyer became involved in the representation of a co-defendant. He approached the case in what was clearly a highly antagonistic and offensive way in the first meeting he attended. Not only was he competitive with the plaintiffs, but he chose this same approach with others in the defense group as well. Richard recognized the danger that this man's approach posed to the progress that our group was making. He quickly challenged this new lawyer in what was a test of advocacy, understanding of the law, pure will, and overall intelligence and did so in a very competitive manner. The antagonistic lawyer became quiet and was not disruptive for the rest of the negotiation. After this display, which was a side of Richard that I had never seen, I asked him why he did it. Richard kindly repeated a line from an old Hill Street Blues show: "—hole lawyers, you got to get them before they get you." While I would not recommend Richard's exact method for addressing a dysfunctional team member because it is not conducive to effective relationship-building, I would emphasize the principle behind the action: the best and most respected lawyers in the room were positive and problem-solving-oriented, and the disruption of the overall effort to accomplish an effective outcome should not be tolerated.

Once a leader has successfully organized a functional team, he or she must effectively motive the team for high levels of performance.

4. Motivation

Motivation is anything that provides direction, intensity, and persistence to behavior.[37] It is essential for achievement of, and the ability to implement, positive change. Leaders cultivate and encourage motivation in their team members in order to further the team's collective goals. However, how does a leader effectively motivate their team?

There are many different ways to motivate, and naturally, some techniques are better suited in certain situations than in others. There has been so much written about motivation and this subject is far beyond the scope of this book. However, leaders who are knowledgeable about different motivational theories are more likely to choose the right motivational tool for an employee or for use in a negotiation. The most successful leaders will look with a critical eye at the circumstances and determine the best motivational technique to employ. Admittedly, this is not easy an easy task because your team members and situations can be different every day.

As Duke's men's basketball Coach K [Krzyzewski] put it in an interview for *Investor's Business Daily*[38]: "Things don't stay the same. You have to understand that not only your business situation changes, but the people you're working with aren't the same day to day. Someone is sick. Someone is having a wedding. [You must] gauge the mood, the thinking level of the team that day." Tom Peters explains that your six-person project team or seven-person training department or 18-person manufacturing unit is a new puzzle every day. It goes far beyond, "treat everybody differently according to their skills. It's that in a 220-day work year, we, the leader-manager, face 220 different teams! Every day is a new crossword puzzle!"[39] The best thing a Leading Lawyer can do is seek out the most appropriate motivational tool that will allow them to draw exceptional work from their individual team members.

a. Motivational Approaches

Satisfaction of Needs: Generally speaking, the first tool of motivation involves the satisfaction of needs. Remember, that not only is a need-satisfaction analysis an important tool with respect to employees and team members, it can also be used to help motivate the opposing side in a negotiation by helping you to understand them and anticipate and meet their needs as well.

Everyone has basic needs and leaders can motivate team members by helping them satisfy those needs. Some may be familiar with Maslow's hierarchy of needs which posits that people are motivated by a hierarchy of five basic needs: physical survival, security, sense of belonging, self-esteem, and self-actualization. Leaders face the challenge of determining what needs have or have not been satisfied in order to properly motivate people.[40] In a typical analysis, one would want to start with meeting lower-level needs and move up toward self-esteem and self-actualization. In this sense, needs can be satisfied by intrinsic factors such as feelings of achievement, recognition, challenge, and advancement which should be kept in mind as a leader designs projects and assigns work. Again, not only are these important for the success of a team, but security and self-esteem are often needs that very much should be met in many areas of conflict.

Another need theory holds that employees are motivated by their need for achievement, power, and affiliation.[41] People who are more achievement-oriented are likely to set higher personal and work goals and are more likely to expend the effort needed to accomplish them.[42] Under this method, leaders

127

need to give high achievers clear goals and provide the resources they need to succeed.

Goal Setting and Process Tools: Other motivational techniques are more process-oriented and focus on understanding how employees behave to fulfill their own needs.[43] For instance, the motivational tool of goal-setting is the most familiar and easiest way to change a team members' behavior. Goals serve to direct attention, mobilize effort, and help people continue exerting effort until the goal is reached. Leaders can help team members by demonstrating how the goal can be attained by following a systematic plan. Commitment to the goal is critical and workers exert the greatest effort when performance is accompanied by feedback. Leaders face the dilemma of deciding how challenging to make the goal and might motivate most effectively by setting moderately difficult goals, recognizing partial goal accomplishment, and making use of a continuous-improvement philosophy by making goals incrementally more difficult.[44]

There is another process theory that asserts that people will be motivated to do a task if three conditions are met: 1) they can perform the task adequately if they put forth enough effort; 2) they will be rewarded if they do it, and 3) they value the reward.[45] This theory involves two fundamental assumptions: first, that motivated performance is the result of conscious choice and second, that people will do what they believe will provide them the highest rewards. A leader can motivate others under this theory by clarifying links between behaviors, performance, and rewards.

Carrot and Stick; Reinforcement Tools: The third category of motivational techniques relies upon team member reinforcement tools. These are the carrot and the stick theories which are basic but effective. The first is the theory of rewards and punishment used to change or reinforce behavior. Research shows that leaders who properly design and implement contingent reward systems increase worker productivity and performance.[46] Leaders should specify what behaviors are important and determine if those behaviors are being rewarded, punished, or ignored. They should also find out what workers find rewarding and punishing and must be aware of creating perceived inequalities when administering individually tailored rewards or punishments. Leaders should not limit themselves to administering organizationally sanctioned rewards and punishments, like a bonus. Social recognition and performance feedback result in productivity improvements as well.[47]

Another reinforcement-based theory suggests that leaders give team members autonomy and latitude in order to increase their motivation for work. Employees are closest to the problem and have the most information and therefore can often make the best decisions. Leaders should equip workers with the resources, knowledge, and skills necessary to make those good decisions. Poor implementation, little guidance and support result in a quick end to this motivational tool if workers start making poor decisions. Training, trust, and time are necessary for this approach to be successful.[48]

Each group of motivational theories answers a different question relating to team member performance[49] and places a strong premium on leader-team communication. Leaders with poor interpersonal communication, feedback, and coaching skills might have a difficult time using these theories.[50] In the same sense, asking questions, listening, and understanding the other side in a negotiation will help you to identify the underlying motivations of the other side in a negotiation. Oftentimes in negotiations, there is the stated reason for a conflict and then there is the "real" reason *behind* the conflict. The real underlying reason is often related to these motivational criteria and understanding them will be beneficial in many negotiations. In team situations, addressing the needs of employees that should be met by their job, understanding how employees choose behavior to fulfill those needs, and acknowledging what team leaders can do to encourage members to behave in ways that meet the firm's objectives are all useful tools that can enhance the success of your team whether it be a small group or the entire organization.

5. Emotional IQ

a. Emotional Quotient v. Intelligence Quotient

A final skill commonly found among Leading Lawyers and effective leaders in general is acute awareness of their emotions and those of others. While most of us are familiar with the idea of an intelligence quotient, more commonly referred to as IQ, not many of us are familiar with the emerging concept of an emotional quotient, referred to as EQ. From the very beginning of our education we are engrained with the notion that our intelligence level is indicated by our ability to perform well on tests and achieve good grades. As a result, it is only natural that we associate a person's potential to succeed with their IQ. However, it is now recognized that while these IQ indicators of academic excellence, intellectual ability, and technical skills are important to success, some would argue that one's EQ is often the greatest indicator of one's potential to succeed.

For example, a national survey of what employers are looking for in entry-level positions indicates that skills associated with IQ do not rank as high as one might think.[51] Employers ranked an ability to learn on the job as the number one desired quality for applicants. Employers have also indicated that it is important for successful applicants to possess an ability to listen, an ability to adapt to different situations, creative problem-solving skills, motivation, confidence, cooperativeness, and a strong desire to make a positive contribution.[52] Of the seven most commonly ranked desirable traits, only one was academic-based; competence in reading, writing, and math.[53]

It seems as though the American workforce may be lacking in these desired EQ skills. In another survey it was found that more than half of employers report that their employees lack the motivation to keep learning and improving on the job; that only four out of 10 employees are able to work cooperatively with their peers; and a minuscule 19% of entry-level employees have the desired amount of self-discipline.[54] These two surveys indicate emotional intelligence is of great value to a job candidate, in addition to academic achievement. Developing the skill of emotional intelligence, which encompasses things such as self-motivation, optimism, and empathy will set you heads and shoulders above your competition.

b. What Is Emotional Intelligence?

Emotional intelligence is a skill that we learn throughout our lives as we become more aware of ourselves and of those around us. A common misconception of emotional intelligence is that having a high emotional intelligence requires you to be "nice" to everybody. Emotional intelligence may dictate firmness with another in order to help them confront a reality which they have been avoiding. Author Daniel Goleman describes emotional intelligence in terms of five key elements: self- awareness, self-regulation, motivation, empathy and social skills.[55] These elements come together to indicate the extent to which a person is attuned to his or her own feelings and the feelings of others.[56] Each of these indicators of emotional intelligence encompasses a distinct skill:

- **Self-Awareness:** examining your own emotions in order to understand how they affect your performance; using your values as a guide in the decision-making process; self-assessing strengths and weakness; and being confident in your abilities.[57]

- **Self-Regulation:** controlling stress, retaining the ability to think clearly under high pressure and in emotionally charged environments; handling impulses well; and exercising self-restraint.[58]

- **Motivation:** enjoying challenging environments; seeking to achieve more, having the ability to take the initiative, being optimistic, and allowing personal preferences to guide your future goals.[59]

- **Empathy:** having the ability to see another's point of view, being culturally aware, behaving openly and honestly, and withholding prejudgment of those persons with whom you are dealing.[60]

- **Social Skills:** Utilizing skills of persuasion such as good communication, listening to others, teamwork, cooperation, negotiation, inspiration of others, and ability to deal with others' emotions. [61]

Emotional intelligence is a skill set, not the state of being emotional. It requires that you manage your emotions, rather than let them control a situation, so that you may work effectively and efficiently toward reaching a common goal. William Loris has a high EQ and has been successful in using those skills to gain support for his projects. He uses his emotions to demonstrate his commitment to a project and the people involved. Loris is aware of his emotions and those of others and he presents his ideas in a way that will best reach his audience, thereby gaining their support.[62] Leading Lawyers are aware of their emotions and those of others and are able to regulate themselves and effectively integrate emotions into rational problem-solving in an appropriate and effective way.

c. There Are Consequences to Low Emotional Intelligence.

When speaking to this issue in a 1994 report on the current state of emotional literacy in the U.S., Goleman stated that "in navigating our lives, it is our fears and envies, our rages and depressions, our worries and anxieties that steer us day to day. Even the most academically brilliant among us are vulnerable to being undone by unruly emotions..."[63] In many situations emotionally charged responses, termed "emotional hijacking" by Goleman, will have disastrous consequences in both the professional and personal arena.[64] We may leave a good deal on the table because we were offended by a remark made during negotiations. We may draw the ill will of a judge if we allow our frustration and anger to dictate our actions in the courtroom. Alternatively we may fail to speak with confidence because we are holding on to past failures. All of these emotional hijackings will result in the polarization of the part of our brain which allows us to think through complex situations and utilize our skills to the best of our ability; therefore, we need to learn and develop the modern survival skills of emotional intelligence.

Every trial lawyer will tell you about the need for high emotional intelligence. In one bench trial, I suffered from an EQ miscalculation when the judge disliked and distrusted my client more than I thought. I choose a bench trial because of my client's "personality" but even the judge, who one might hope would detach his emotions from his decision-making, disliked him. It was an uphill battle that did not turn out as I had hoped. I should have been more aware of how others saw my client even though I felt he was telling the truth.

d. Developing Your Emotional Intelligence

Once you are able to self-regulate emotional reactions and avoid emotional hijackings, you can begin to develop a broad range of skills to build or improve your emotional intelligence. Developing emotional intelligence means becoming emotionally literate, acknowledging the emotions in a situation, and showing empathy for those with whom you are working.

The skill of emotional literacy involves the way in which we attempt to express or identify our emotions. Many times we could benefit by labeling our emotions, rather than labeling people or situations. Emotional literacy will allow you to appropriately identify your emotions which will in turn help you to communicate your concern, frustration, or fear and help de-escalate a conflict situation. By appropriately identify our concerns, rather than waging a personal attack, we are much more likely to come to reach a common goal. If you act out your anger by placing blame on the other party, they will likely react with either anger or aversion to the problem. If you identify (or in counseling terms) take possession of your emotions, the person with whom you are communicating will be more willing to work toward reaching a common solution. In a professional setting, this does not mean that you simply expose your emotions. Identifying them for your own categorization and understanding them is the important step.

Keep in mind and acknowledge the importance of emotions in a situation. One common way of evaluating a dilemma is to make a list of pros and cons which allows for an objective assessment of the benefits and drawbacks of each potential course of action. In addition to tangible concerns that each decision will require for implementation, such as economic outcome, risk, time, and effort, we should consider how each potential outcome will make our clients, and the opposition, feel as well. Although lawyers are often reluctant to ask about emotional or personal matters, it can be very important to both client relationships and the deal-making process to ask these kinds of questions.[65] Lawyers need to keep in mind that by the time a client arrives at his or her door, he or she is often in a very emotional state. Strong emotions are going to be present, and a lawyer can establish a good client relationship by first acknowledging the presence and effects of those emotions.

Finally, a lawyer can move forward in addressing emotions by showing empathy. Empathy is defined as the having the ability to recognize moods and emotions of others and having the ability to perceive how others are reacting to your emotions and behavior.[66] In order to show empathy, you first need to really listen. Most clients, on both sides, will be more than willing to tell you about their frustration and fears if you are willing to listen. Next, it is important to reiterate to a client that you understand the way that they feel. Showing empathy and understanding toward your client will help the client to feel more comfortable and help to form a trusting relationship which will lead to a more productive relationship. When you are negotiating or in settlement discussions it can be beneficial for you and your client to show a certain degree of empathy toward the other side. In order to come to an agreement, you must necessarily satisfy some of the other party's interests, therefore, it is imperative to understand what is important to the other side and more critically why it is important. By understanding the other side's perspective, you will be better able to find value-creating trades and avoid impasses in negotiations.[67]

In order to integrate emotional intelligence into effective leadership, you need to be able to perceive your surrounding circumstances and decide which emotional intelligence skills will make you the most effective leader in that particular situation. Being an emotionally intelligent Leading Lawyer requires that you perceive a situation and integrate your emotional understanding of yourself and others in order to decide how you can induce the desired change.

6. Conclusion

Leading Lawyers know that dealing effectively with the human elements of conflict, building relationships, and collaborating as teams are essential elements of success. One can ignore these issues at their peril. Furthermore, the most successful lawyers, just like the "star" scientist at Bell Laboratory, are aware that trading favors, empathizing with people, and facilitating the smooth operation of group dynamics will pay off in innumerable ways. We all know that a group is stronger than its individual parts and Leading Lawyers rely upon others to advance their and their clients causes. Leading Lawyers depend upon positive relationships in order to better advance their client's position and provide them greater benefits and rewards.[68]

———

Notes

[1.] Mr. Charan has an MBA, PhD. from Harvard and was a Harvard Business School faculty member. His first book was *Execution*, co-authored with Larry Bossidy, which has sold over 2 million copies.

[2.] Ram Charan, *Know How: The 8 Skills that Separate People Who Perform from those Who Don't*, Crown Business (2007).

[3.] John H. Zenger and Joseph Folkman, *Extraordinary Leaders: Turning Good Managers into Great Leaders*, 182-183 McGraw-Hill (2002).

[4.] Curt Grayson and David Baldwin, *Leadership Networking: Connect, Collaborate, Create*, 9 (2007).

[5.] *Id.* at 11.

[6.] *Id.* at 14.

[7.] Rajesh Setty, *Lasting Relationships*, 12 (2006), *available at* www.rajeshsetty.com.

[8.] Grayson and Baldwin, *supra* note 4 at 15.

[9.] *Id.* at 16.

[10.] *The Lawyer Transatlantic Elite*, ed. Catrin Griffiths, 15 (2008), http://cde.cerosmedia.com/1X482757614712f012.cde.

[11.] Interview with Larry Sonsini, August 2006.

[12.] David Gergen, "The Spirit of Teamwork", *U.S. News & World Report, available at* www.usnews.com/articles/news/best-leaders/2007/11/12/united-they-stand (accessed March 9, 2008).

[13.] *See* G. Richard Shell, *Bargaining for Advantage*, Viking Press (1999).

[14.] Interview with Leon Panetta, October 2006.

15. *Id.*

16. Bret Schulte, *U.S. News & World Report* (November 2007).

17. Interview with Leon Panetta, October 2006.

18. Richard L. Hughes, Robert C. Ginnett and Gordon J. Curphy, *Leadership: Enhancing the Lessons of Experience* 24 McGraw-Hill (5th ed. 2006).

19. Andre Martin, What's Next?: The 2007 Changing Nature of Leadership Survey, 14, available at www.ccl.org.

20. James S. Kouzes and Barry Z. Posner, *The Leadership Challenge,* 224 Jossey-Bass (4th ed. 2007).

21. Interview with Deborah Garza, August 2008.

22. *Id.*

23. Interview with Justice Joyce Kennard, August 2008.

24. M.K. Smith, (2005) "Bruce W. Tuckman - forming, storming, norming and performing in groups", *the encyclopedia of informal education,* www.infed.org/thinkers/tuckman.htm.

25. Bruce Tuckman, "Developmental Sequence in Small Groups", *Psychological Bulletin,* 63, 384-399 (1965).

26. Hughes, Ginnett and Curphy, *supra* note 18 at 305-306.

27. Kouzes and Posner, *surpa* note 20 at 227.

28. *Id.* at 229.

29. *Id.* at 221.

30. *Id.*

31. *Id.* at 233.

32. Interview with Robert Grey, July 2008.

33. Kouzes and Posner, *supra* note 20 at 237.

34. *Id.*

35. Stephanie Powell, "eBusiness marketing manager at Plantronics" in Kouzes and Posner, *supra* note 20 at 240.

36. Hughes, Ginnett and Curphy, *surpa* note 18 at 299-300.

37. *Id.* at 243.

38. *Investor's Business Daily,* (November 10, 2006), http://www.investors.com/.

39. Tom Peters, *The Ultimate Daily Crossword Puzzle* (November 14, 2006), http://www.tom-peters.com/entries.php?note=009384.php.

40. Hughes, Ginnett and Curphy, *supra* note 18 at 250-251.

41. Robert N. Lussier and Christopher F. Achua, *Leadership: Theory, Application, Skill Development* 75, South Western College Pub. (2nd ed. 2004).

42. Hughes, Ginnett and Curphy, *supra* note 18 at 253.

43. Lussier and Achua, *supra* note 41 at 75.

44. Hughes, Ginnett and Curphy, *supra* note 18 at 259-261.

45. *Id.* at 262.

46. *Id.* at 269.

47. *Id.*

48. *Id.* at 272.

49. Lussier and Achua, *supra* note 41 at 51.

50. Hughes, Ginnett and Curphy, *supra* note 18 at 267.

51. Daniel Goleman, *Working With Emotional Intelligence*, 12-13 Bantam Books (1998).

52. *Id.* at 13.

53. *Id.*

54. *Id.* at 12.

55. Daniel Goleman, *Emotional Intelligence*, (December 2001), http://www.managers.org.uk/doc_docs/THK-0531334.pdf (accessed October 10, 2006).

56. Gary Yukl, *Leadership in Organizations*, Prentice Hall (5th ed. 2002).

57. Goleman, *supra* note 55.

58. *Id.*

59. *Id.*

60. *Id.*

61. *Id.*

62. Interview with William T. Loris, April 2007.

63. "Emotional Understanding", http://www.funderstanding.com/eq.cfm.

64. Goleman, *supra* note 55 at 75.

65. Robert H. Mnookin, *Beyond Winning: Negotiating to Create Value in Deals and Disputes*, 184 The Belknap Press of Harvard University Press (2000).

66. Yukl, *supra* note 56 at 196.

67. Mnookin, *supra* note 65 at 180-181.

68. Lussier and Achua, *supra* note 41 at 261.

CHAPTER EIGHT:
Leadership Is the Future of the Profession

Generally speaking, lawyers today are meeting the needs of their clients by legal, business, political, and social standards and the bar and bench have remained on par with society's issues. However, lawyers realize that as a profession we have fallen under the harsh light of scrutiny. While we can point to other fields that share in this negative limelight (including bankers and accountants) and we know that countless industries have dealt with issues of unlawful and immoral activity, the reality is that, as of late, there has been much discussion and criticism targeted at the legal profession. However, there is great opportunity for the progression of the legal profession through the development of leadership and entrepreneurial roles in our organizations, in conjunction with a strong moral authority that will provide the occasion for positive social and commercial change. We lawyers are continuing to improve and, to borrow a phrase from Kouzes and Posner: this is our *Leadership Challenge*. We can expand the services we provide to our clients, communities, nonprofit, and nongovernmental agencies by facilitating positive and ethical change. In accomplishing these tasks, we can ensure a loyal clientele, create excellent reputations, *and* develop social and entrepreneurial opportunities.

"I really think that lawyers of my vintage need to think about a legacy, our legacy, which means the kind of lawyers we're leaving behind us. We need to worry about helping young lawyers to develop. These lawyers coming up are our legacy."

Deborah Garza
Deputy Assistant Attorney General for the U.S. Department of Justice

"We as lawyers are best suited to improve the human conditions under which we all live, whether it's for the environment, whether it's for human rights, whether it's for economic development, or cultural sustainability. Lawyers are in the best position to help improve these conditions in concert with others."

Robert Grey
Former President of the American Bar Association

1. A Look at Our Tradition

For decades, the legal profession was something to which people aspired, and certainly many still do. Our practitioners were revered as pillars of society and not because of clever marketing; the image was attributable to the roles that lawyers played in their communities and the values they espoused and upheld.

Mary Ann Glendon, a Harvard law professor and author, wrote in her book *A Nation Under Lawyers*, that "[t]raditionally, the country has depended on the legal profession to supply most of our needs for consensus builders, problem solvers, troubleshooters, dispute avoiders and dispute settlers...The country's need for talented people in these roles is greater than it has ever been. The opportunities for satisfaction and a sense of personal accomplishment are unparalleled."[2] Lawyers have been pointed to as *peacemakers*, even in litigation. The goal was not to make the other side exhaust their resources but to reach a compromise. Winning at all costs was not a preferred solution. "...[C]ompromise whenever you can....As a peacemaker, a lawyer has a superior opportunity of being a good [human being]."[3]

Once there were so many powerful and favorable images of lawyers that Walter Bennett, a North Carolina lawyer and writer, easily documented them in his book, *The Lawyers Myth*. The traditional roles of lawyers conjured noble images. Bennett stresses the importance of what those lawyers signified and how they shaped the community's attitudes. The reality is important, but so too are aspirations; they help shape the reality. Bennett focuses on the head start that lawyers have on what we are calling leadership behavior. "To serve greater society, the legal profession must resurrect its own community...We need the vision of service to the greater community in order to develop a moral consensus on professional values, and we need a professional community bound by common values in order to envision a higher purpose ..."[4]

One of these positive images that Bennett identified was that of the *lawyer-statesman*. Its crux was a willingness to elevate the public good to the highest virtue. "[T]he ideal was the lodestar for the well-loved life of the public man," Bennett writes. "Today that ideal has been overshadowed by the rising specters of high-priced lobbyists, political operatives, and good-lawyers-gone-bad."[5] As Yale Law School Professor Anthony Kronman writes in his book, *The Lost Lawyer*: "The lawyer-statesman ideal... calls upon the lawyer who adopts it not just to acquire a set of intellectual skills, but to develop certain character traits as well." This includes being calm and cautious, sympathizing with conflicting view points, good judgment which include both expertise, and character virtue, prudence, and practical wisdom.[6]

There was also the ideal of the *pillar of the community*. This was the local courthouse version of the lawyer-statesman: widely respected for character, active in civic affairs, a linchpin of the community. "[A] lawyer's calling was thus far beyond that of legal technician and courtroom operator," Bennett says. Their work "was ultimately tied to…relationships between people, between people and businesses, and between people and their government. On the local level, a lawyer was the glue that held all of that together and the grease that made it work."[7] Abraham Lincoln, before his election to Congress as an Illinois attorney launched him toward lawyer-statesmanship, was the prototype of the pillar of the community, according to Bennett.

Another popular image was the lawyer as a *champion of people and causes*. This is the crusading activist, from Daniel Webster to the fictional Atticus Finch of *To Kill a Mockingbird* and beyond. Bennett says the exemplar of champion of people and causes is Thurgood Marshall who, before reaching the Supreme Court, successfully argued *Brown v. Board of Education*. The image of this ideal has since faded. Bennett believes it has been tarnished badly by O.J. Simpson's "Dream Team" and similar courtroom spectacles. Barnett also highlights how the lawyer was once seen as a *paragon of virtue and rectitude* and the *conscience of the community*. This includes judges who represent "a sure morality that transcends even the law they are sworn to uphold,'[8] the proverbial incorruptible district attorneys, and lawyers who refuse to represent a cause they regard as immoral, or conversely, lawyers who stand up to the community and take unpopular cases at considerable cost to themselves. Lawyers had a reputation for representing both people and causes that were deserving of advocacy. This is the archetype that Bennett sees having suffered the most of all: "[M]any people do not recognize or do not credit the virtuous lawyer now in any form."[9]

Finally, there is the *lawyer and gentleman*. Bennett describes this ideal as a combination of the *paragon of virtue* with "keen intelligence, well-practiced skills, and a willingness to work very hard."[10] A lawyer with all of these qualities could be not only highly regarded, powerful, and virtuous, but attain personal wealth. Bennett sees the *lawyer and gentleman* personified in John W. Davis, one of the leading appellate lawyers of the 20th century who argued 140 cases before the Supreme Court and held the Democratic presidential nomination in the race against incumbent Calvin Coolidge. Mr. Davis was someone with "extraordinary charm and adopted the gentlemanly principles of honesty, propriety, courtesy and fairdealing". [11]

These once iconic images of the members of the legal profession, for better or worse have faded, if not disappeared in today's society. Casual research reveals and chronicles the various criticisms of lawyers and the profession as a whole. Because many of the criticisms have undeniable merit, it is important to acknowledge and understand them in order to change the behavior that prompted them.

2. Criticisms of the Profession

The most comprehensive and objective accounts of the history and current state of the legal profession have come from our own ranks. Books written by Sol Linowitz, cofounder and chairman of the Xerox Corporation, Presidential Medal of Honor Recipient, and partner with Coudert Brothers in Washington, D.C.; former dean of Yale Law School Anthony Kronman; UCLA Law Professor Richard Abel; and Harvard Law professor Mary Ann Glendon, recount the grand roots of the legal profession and point to the high-profile roles that lawyers fill in today's society. However, they also take stock of the common and concern-inducing criticisms of the legal profession and provide suggestions on how to get the profession back on track.

The criticisms of the legal profession and its members span an array of concerns. One such concern is that those of the legal profession have suffered a loss of humanity[12] and put an emphasis on rights and obligations over maintaining relationships. Another criticism, that has historical roots yet persists today, points to a marked drive toward winning over compromise; also referred to as the "scorched earth" or take-no-prisoners approach to litigation. David Lubin in his article calls this adversarial ruthlessness.[13] Lord Brougham, Chancellor of the United Kingdom in the 1830s, made this statement about how lawyers perform services for their client:

> An advocate, in the discharge of his duty, knows but one person in all the world and that person is his client. To save that client, by all means and expedients, and at all hazards and costs to other persons, and, among them, to himself, is his first and only duty; and in performing this duty he must not

*regard the alarm, the torments, the destruction which he may
bring upon others.*[14]

The modern equivalent to Lord Brougham's point of view is that "lawyers
are hired guns; they know they are, their clients demand that they be and the
public sees them that way..."[15]

Related is a view that lawyers are no longer independent and objective
professionals.[16] Linowitz holds that a professional who can make their own
decisions about what they will or will not do are more worthy of respect than
people who are always ready to do what they are told.[17] Mayor Giuliani says
that leadership means dealing with a client "so that you become more than
just a reflection of your client." [18] Professor Abel and his colleagues deny a
meaningful professionalism to those who remain autonomous in selecting their
means but only by allowing others to determine their goals.[19]

The outcry is that lawyers are amoral and are willing to argue their client's
position without regard to whether the outcome is ethical or within the spirit
of the law. Authors Richard Zitrin and Carol Langford write in their book,
The Moral Compass of the American Lawyer, that: the "adversary theorem"
and our duties to our clients create a palpable tension between the rules of
legal ethics and other important principles of our society: telling the truth,
being fair and compassionate, seeking justice, being courageous, acting as a
moral human being. While the public looks to the legal system for the truth,
lawyers often look to spin the truth from their client's perspective.[20] They later
describe two criminal defense lawyers who failed to reveal the whereabouts
of a murdered young woman's body because the lawyers felt it their duty to
protect their serial killer client. The community in which the murder took place
was outraged.

Critics also assert that the legal profession has become commercialized and
that lawyers are driven for the best clients and highest fees.[21] Others simply describe it as greed.[22] Linowitz comments that "what seems to characterize the
perceived leadership of the profession is too often not a reputation for public
service, probity, judgment or scholarship but a reputation for representing the
biggest clients and charging the highest fees."[23] Mary Ann Glendon points to
the effects of this trend on the operation of a traditional law firm by highlighting that the motivation of profit-making:

> *....also resulted in the changing of the rules of the law*
> *firm. Many people in the 70's entered the profession with the*
> *idea that talent and hard work were all they needed to suc-*
> *ceed. In the 70's, that relative comfortable situation began*
> *to change as a result of more competition and economic re-*
> *alities. For associates and partners, the idea that partnership*
> *was a lifelong relationship ended. Compensation changed to*
> *a productivity-based system providing more incentives to the*
> *business getter.[24]*

The former president of the Canadian Bar Association feels the same and was quoted as saying, "Not very long ago a lawyer was more than a human punch clock churning out billable time units."[25] As Anthony Kronman points out, "[t]he concept of character and integrity are not essential to a commercial model of practice."[26]

Another consequence of the practice of law operating more like a business is what some critics believe is a loss of public trust. Former federal judge Simon Rifkind, who entered the profession in the '30s and was still practicing law in '90s, once commented that "[t]he advocate has more than a private fiduciary relationship with a client; he also has a public trust..."[27] Elihu Root, a great lawyer and Secretary of War and Secretary of State under President McKinley who also won the Nobel Peace Prize in 1912, believed that "[a]bout half the practice of a decent lawyer consists in telling would-be clients that they are damned fools and should stop."[28] Because the public has recognized a drive in the legal profession to secure the highest fees, the trust that a lawyer will provide this advice when necessary is waning. Society counts on the law, and on lawyers as its ambassadors, to spread feelings of trust throughout the community. Instead, too often, we help weaken them.[29] Previously, the law had been seen as a helping profession, not a continuation of war by other means for a profit. [30]

Furthermore, there are character traits that lawyers tend to have in common that have been singled out critically. In his article "Herding Cats: The Lawyer Personality Revealed," Larry Richard found several specific ways that lawyers are distinct from other people. He asserts that lawyers are skeptical. Lawyers score in the *90th percentile* of the population for skepticism according to the Caliper Profile, a leading personality assessment. "People who score high on this trait tend to be...cynical, judgmental, questioning, argumentative and somewhat self-protective."[31] Richard's research also placed lawyers in the 89th percentile for a group that desires autonomy. "They like to work independently and may resist working collaboratively with others."[32] Lastly, Richard concludes that lawyers are often impatient. When it comes to "urgency," lawyers score in the 71st percentile. This relates to "impatience, a need to get things done, a sense of immediacy...Urgent people are sometimes brusque, poor listeners..."[33] Those who score low on urgency, on the other hand, "tend to be patient, contemplative, measured ...."[34]

Admittedly, on an individual and personal level, lawyers sometimes demonstrate characteristics that, while useful in certain situations, are not generally viewed as positive traits and are even seen as harmful in some circumstances. Lawyers have created (as a result of a competitive economy) a far more commercial profession than it has been in years past. In litigation, we strive toward winning and consequently, litigation has become more expensive. In this profit-seeking environment, the humanitarian lawyer is reduced in stature and in priority. The business-oriented lawyer has emerged and commercial priorities have come to outweigh social concerns. *Likewise, this is our current reality.*

However, the most successful lawyers have learned to *enhance* this reality. They realize that it is possible to improve and prosper in this new environment if you accept the past *and* acknowledge and transform the future. Leading Lawyers have moved toward the inevitable commercial practice but one is driven by leadership and positive change. They incorporate our longstanding professional traits and traditions with the best leadership ideas: ethical innovation and relationship-oriented entrepreneurial thinking. Leading Lawyers rely upon their professionalism, expertise, and judgment as they guide their client's commercial interests, their organization, and communities into the future. Leadership and the essential values and commercial realities of our profession are wholly complementary.

The model of the Leading Lawyer is a conjunctive one. Incorporating the skills of a traditional advocacy-driven lawyer with the skills of leader provides us with a promising future. Practicing leadership and the law creates a powerful combination for professional, organizational, and community progress. Moreover, leadership skills are becoming increasingly indispensable. The Leading Lawyer will become the new commercial reality *because our clients will demand it.* The profession will become more entrepreneurial, driving down costs and improving systems and transactions. We will actively help the court system, nonprofit organizations, and NGOs to achieve positive change rather than clog them with competitive and noncollaborative behavior, again, because *our clients will reward this behavior*. In due time, those legal organizations that instill leadership, train for innovation, and challenge themselves to improve their business and social communities will thrive; those that do not, will not.

The less than perfect image of the legal profession is now a cliché. There is a cultural medium for unflattering images of lawyers. As a group, and individually, we are all concerned about the attitudes toward our profession in the communities in which we live. However, the current, unfavorable images of lawyers were not always the norm. We have the ability to change how we are viewed by changing how we operate.

All of these historical ideals and present tarnished images of lawyers allow us to fully understand where we currently stand as a profession. In today's world, how do we return to our traditions and but remain competitive? How do we make those ideals current and functional in our new commercial world? Lawyers must move beyond the frivolous, purely competitive, needless litigation and reinstate themselves as leaders of positive and ethical change. Already we are gazing back nostalgically at the past legends of iconic lawyers that may sound like a fairy tale to young lawyers today. We can do better by creating a new legacy founded in leadership and that is the challenge for the future of the legal profession.

3. Creating a Lasting Legacy

Kouzes and Posner wrote in their book *A Leader's Legacy* that "[e]ach of us, whether we intend to or not, will become at some point a character in someone's story." [35] This simple statement highlights the significance of a legacy and begs an important question; what do people say about us now and what will they say when we are gone? However, this is not just a question for more experienced lawyers; thinking about the direction of their careers is something Leading Lawyers perform early in their careers. As Deborah Garza points out, "Every interaction that we have as young lawyers, we're building our relationships. We're demonstrating our strengths and our weaknesses".[36]

Thinking about the kind of legacy you want to leave can never begin too early in your career and can be an extremely energizing and uplifting process.[37] It forces you to think about your actions today in a larger context.[38] Legacies encompass the past, present, and future. When pondering your legacies, consider where you have been, where you are now, and where you see yourself headed.[39] Leading Lawyers seek to develop positive ideas that result in positive action; their consistent positive actions result in positive habits; positive habits result in a positive character; and a positive character establishes a lasting legacy.[40] For instance, when he took office as president of the American Bar Association, Robert Grey decided that he wanted to leave a legacy of improving the judicial system through improvement of the American jury system. Through a collaborative effort with a group of distinguished colleagues, Grey created a campaign titled *Better Justice, Better Jury* designed to raise the bar for what it means to serve on a jury. The project was aimed at assisting state and local bar associations and courts in understanding the need to make it easier for people to report for jury duty when called, make it convenient and comfortable while they wait, aid their understanding of the evidence once they are selected, help them reach well-reasoned and fair verdicts, and protect their privacy along the way. Like Robert Grey, take responsibility for your actions with the realization that those actions have consequences, if not immediate, then certainly for the future.[41] Leave the kind of legacy that you intend to leave instead of an accidental and unintended one.[42]

It is important to understand that our colleagues will decide whether or not they want to remember us and walk in our footsteps.[43] No matter how much formal power or authority our positions give us, we will only leave a lasting legacy if others want to mirror our work ethic, operate at the same level of integrity, and persist with the vision of positive change.[44] Leaving a legacy that subsequent lawyers will want to continue requires dedicating ourselves to making a difference, not just working to achieve fame and fortune.[45] It also means appreciating that others will inherit what we leave behind.[46]

4. The Challenge of Leadership

The legal profession will continue to be a commercial enterprise and will fully embrace the leadership principles that have already been adopted by our corporate clients, community leaders, and social entrepreneurs. The most successful legal institutions will educate for character improvement and make it part of their culture. Our clients will require us to learn and practice the skills of leadership. Eventually, our institutions will train for character improvement beyond mere compliance with the law. They will train for innovation, creative thinking, collaboration, and team building. Lawyers will continue to be *legal experts*, but they will also improve their values as well as their social and commercial entrepreneurial behavior. I further predict that law schools will slowly begin to teach creative problem solving and perhaps a leadership model in *parallel* to the advocacy model. They will teach that advocacy is necessary in criminal litigation and perhaps in civil litigation but that problem-solving and collaboration is preferred for the lion's share of legal work that a majority of lawyers perform on a daily basis.

In the commercial world, Leading Lawyers will be value-driven and entrepreneurial. In the nonprofit world, they will be social entrepreneurs.[47] We will continue to move away from a purely advocacy-based system in many areas of the law. To some extent, I agree with David Luban who criticizes lawyers who use the adversary system as an excuse for ruthlessness in all legal situations.[48] He argues that 'adversarial ruthlessness' as a blanket policy is *justified* only in criminal and quasi criminal defense cases. As a practitioner, I believe that adversarial ruthlessness as a blanket policy is *useful* only in criminal and quasi-criminal defense cases. In most other situations, practitioners will move away from the adversarial system, for purposes of commercial success, client satisfaction, and our legal profession's desire for continued improvement and opportunities.

Lawyers today can build upon a wide base of traditions. Law organizations will improve because their clients are already practicing leadership. They will train their young lawyers to be excellent practitioners *and* fine leaders. Law schools will teach leadership skills; bar associations will educate their constituents; law firms and law departments will train their members for small "l" and big "L" leadership situations. All of this will be done because that is what our clients, organizations, and society require of us. These skills are no longer elective, but are necessary to economic and entrepreneurial advantage in our new economy.

Adversarial ruthlessness is a mindset that has had a corrosive effect on our profession and our personal reputations. It grinds up time, trees, value, and nerves. It burns out many practitioners who flee the profession; and those who stick with it until retirement suffer along the way (lawyers have some of the highest stress levels and divorce levels in the country[49]). The leadership model is different. It is a model directed toward personal and civic virtue, but just as importantly, it is aimed at commercial success and client satisfaction.

The most successful lawyers practice law and leadership and the success of one's institution will depend on them practicing it well. We are fine advocates, great analysts, and the profession is full of outstanding problem-solvers. Leadership is our direction, our future, our calling. Leadership is an *imperative*; it is our *challenge*. We already think and act like lawyers; Leading Lawyers also think and act like leaders.

Notes

1. James Kouzes and Posner, *The Leadership Challenge*, 27 Jossey-Bass (4th ed. 2007).

2. Sol Linowitz, *The Betrayed Profession*, 14 Charles Scribners's Son (1994).

3. Walter Bennett, *The Lawyers Myth*, 136 University of Chicago Press (2001).

4. *Id.* at 29.

5. *Id.* at 16.

6. *Id.* at 33.

7. *Id.* at 39-46.

8. *Id.* at 45.

9. *Id.* at 46.

10. *Id.* at 48.

11. Linowitz, *supra* note 2 at 9.

12. The Fundamental Dilemma of Lawyering: The Ethics of the Hired Gun, Ed. Richard L. Abel, New Press (1997).

13. Henry Peter Brougham, 1st Baron Brougham and Vaux (1778 - 1868) was a British statesman who became Lord Chancellor of the United Kingdom.

14. Linowitz, *supra* note 2 at 10.

15. *Id.* at 24.

16. *Id.*

17. Interview with Rudolf Giuliani, August 2008.

18. Linowitz, *supra* note 2 at 24.

19. Richard Zitrin and Carol Langford, *The Moral Compass of the American Lawyer*, 3 Ballentine Books (1999).

20. Linowitz, *surpa* note 2 at 22.

21. Zitrin and Langford, *supra* note 19.

22. Linowitz, *supra* note 2 at 23.

23. Mary Ann Glendon, *A Nation Under Lawyers*, 20-25 Harvard Press (1994).

24. John R. R. Jennings, "The Bottom Line", *New York State Bar Journal*, 45 (November 1990).

25. Anthony T. Kronman, *The Lost Lawyer*, 356 Belknap Harvard (1993).

26. Linowitz, *supra* note 2.

27. Glendon, *supra* note 23 at 37.

28. Linowitz, *supra* note 2 at 5.

29. *Id.* at 3.

30. Larry R. Richard, *Herding Cats: The Lawyer Personality Revealed, at* http://www.lawmarketing.com/pages/articles.asp?Action=Article&ArticleCategoryID=7&ArticleID=350 (accessed January 9, 2005).

31. *Id.*

32. *Id.*

33. *Id.*

34. Kouzes and Posner, *supra* note 1 at 25.

35. Interview with Deborah Garza, July 2008.

36. Kouzes and Posner, *supra* note 1 at 4.

37. *Id.*

38. *Id.* at 5.

39. John Stott, *Only One Way: The Message of Galatians*, London: Inter-Varsity (1968).

40. Kouzes and Posner, *supra* note 1 at 4.

41. *Id.*

42. *Id.* at 48.

43. *Id.*

44. *Id.* at 5.

45. *Id.*

46. Sarah H. Alvord, L. David Brown and Christine W. Letts, *Social Entrepreneurship: Leadership that Facilitates Societal Transformation—An Exploratory Study*, Harvard Center for Public Leadership.

47. *The Fundamental Dilemma of Lawyering: The Ethics of the Hired Gun*, Ed. Richard L. Abel, New Press (1997).

48. Susan Swaim Daicoff, *Lawyer Know Thyself*, 113 American Psychological Association (2004).

INDEX